THE KINDNESS DIARIES

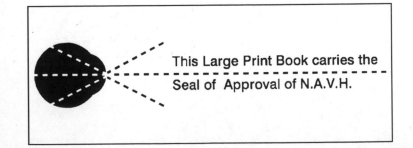

This Large Print Book carries the
Seal of Approval of N.A.V.H.

THE KINDNESS DIARIES

ONE MAN'S QUEST TO IGNITE GOODWILL AND TRANSFORM LIVES AROUND THE WORLD

LEON LOGOTHETIS

THORNDIKE PRESS
A part of Gale, Cengage Learning

GALE
CENGAGE Learning·

Farmington Hills, Mich • San Francisco • New York • Waterville, Maine
Meriden, Conn • Mason, Ohio • Chicago

GALE
CENGAGE Learning

LIBRARY OF CONGRESS CATALOGING-IN-PUBLICATION DATA

Logothetis, Leon.
  [Amazing adventures of a nobody]
  The kindness diaries : one man's quest to ignite goodwill and transform lives around the world / by Leon Logothetis. — Large print edition.
    pages cm. — (Thorndike Press large print inspirational)
    ISBN 978-1-4104-7790-3 (hardcover) — ISBN 1-4104-7790-8 (hardcover)
  1. Logothetis, Leon—Travel—United States. 2. United States—Description and travel—Anecdotes. 3. Conduct of life. 4. Kindness. 5. Large print books. I. Title.
  E169.Z83L64 2015
  177'.7—dc23   2014048740

Published in 2015 by arrangement with Reader's Digest Associates, Inc.

Printed in Mexico
1 2 3 4 5 6 7 19 18 17 16 15

I dedicate this book to every dream
you've ever had . . .
and the one you never knew
you did.

All gifts mentioned in this book have been given to their recipients.

INTRODUCTION

"Act as if what you do makes a
difference. It does."
— William James

I wasn't sure if it was the screaming that
woke me up, or the rather large man standing above me, but either way, I was awake.
In that moment I realized my decision to
sleep on the mean streets of Pittsburgh
might not have been the wisest. But often
my worst decisions had led to my greatest
experiences. It was by saying yes to adventures (especially the crazy ones) that I found
myself in those blood-pumping, soul-
expanding moments of life.

I looked around the dirty, gum-stained
sidewalk on which I had been invited to
sleep. Tony, my new friend and host, was
also now awake, as Richard, the man pacing
between our makeshift beds, yelled at no
one in particular, "I don't feel safe here!"

9

I had just arrived in Pittsburgh that afternoon. I had nothing in my pocket and was relying solely on the kindness of strangers for food, shelter, and gas to make it across the world. That's right, *the world.* After looking for a place to stay all day, I had headed over to a local park, the kind where old men play chess while younger men deal drugs. But Tony was neither. He was just a good man who had fallen on hard times. When I asked him if I could stay with him that night, he had responded with a sad smile, "You could if I wasn't homeless."

And that's how I woke up from sleeping on the streets, in the rain, with a man standing above my bed, screaming that he didn't feel safe. He wasn't alone. I pulled up my ratty blanket to fight the chill — cold and tired and, well, let's face it, a little more than mildly scared. You might as well have frozen a camera on my face and heard my inner voice scream: "Why on earth am I doing this?"

Which I must admit wasn't a bad question. The truth was I was having an existential crisis. It wasn't my first. In fact, it wasn't even my second. I tend to get existential crises as often as other people file their taxes. About once a year I seem to be struck with the feeling that, though life might look rosy on the outside — health, wealth, and friends — things were feeling pretty murky within.

It's been a few years now since I suffered the "Big Kahuna" of existential crises. You see, I used to be someone else. I was living in London working as a successful broker in a family-run business. I was completely uninspired, deeply depressed, and however hard it is to admit, at my darkest times, suicidal. I had little hope for myself, and even less for the world I called home. Then it happened. I stumbled across the film *The Motorcycle Diaries,* which chronicled the inspirational journey of Che Guevara as he crossed South America relying solely on the kindness of strangers. His story lit up my mundane existence.

Here was a romanticized version of the legendary revolutionary connecting with people. Living. Exploring. I wasn't quite ready to overthrow the Cuban government, but I did want to start a revolution of sorts. I wanted to revolt against the predetermined structure of my own life. In Che, I saw a man who was living his dream, a fully realized, *absolutely free* human being. Someone I wished to be. In the moments after the credits of the film had rolled into the ether, I knew something inside me had irrevocably changed. Che was *my* proof that there was more to this little trip on planet Earth. Much more.

Over the next few weeks I found the courage to rise from my slumber. I gave up my comfortable life to travel the world. The apex of those travels was walking across America with only $5 in my pocket and the generosity of strangers making up for the rest. This ultimately led to my first TV show and book *Amazing Adventures of a Nobody*. I left the cold dreary streets of London and moved to Los Angeles: the city of dreams. And to a certain extent, I *was* living my dream. Or at least more than I had been before — I had a lovely girlfriend (Lina), a very friendly dog (Winston), and a job that most days kept me busy. I thought my existential crisis had been resolved, but maybe it had only taken on a different face.

Though I had gone out into the world, changed my life, and brought back some stories, there was still something within me that felt trapped. I felt like I was waking up every morning to live someone else's life, to do someone else's job. I was once again wearing an old familiar mask.

I had a collection of those masks. We all do. Whether you're a young mother in a Belizean jungle or a businessman on the streets

of Manhattan, we each have some preconceived notion about what kind of life we
think we're supposed to live, and then we
become trapped in that perception. We give
up on a childhood dream, or we exchange it
for something that feels safer, more grown
up. I was no different. But even after I shook
off that first mask in London — the mask
of playing it safe — and made my away
across America on $5 a day, I learned that
there were still many masks hiding beneath.
And then one afternoon I found myself
walking down Hollywood Boulevard, and
my whole life changed . . . again.

I had gone out to lunch and was walking
back to my car when it happened. The palm
trees stood out in the distance; the sun beat
down on the star-lined sidewalk; and then I
saw him. He was sitting by an over-packed
grocery cart with a dirty baseball cap on his
head, torn jeans, and a grime-stained face.
But in his hands, the homeless man held a
sign that stopped me dead in my tracks.
Some people might call these moments
turning points. I am one of those people.
And I'm always aware when they happen.
It's as though the world comes to a stand-
still, the orchestra of sounds and words and
cars and life fade into a quiet hum, and the
moment gets etched so deeply into my

memory, I can always feel it right there, under my skin. My face softened as I read the sign in the homeless man's hands. It said, "Kindness is the best medicine."

Here's the funny thing about getting everything you *think* you want. You always want more. But for me, I didn't want more money or more fame. Throughout my previous "amazing adventures," I had gotten a taste of connecting with people in a way I never thought possible. I had made friendships. Real, deep friendships. Our connections were based on more than where we lived or what we did for work; they were about two humans trying to make it through this crazy world. Together.

I realized that I was missing the one thing that had brought me here: connecting with people through the language of kindness. And I don't just mean big, life-changing, "Whoa, did that just happen?" kindness. I also mean the small whispers, the quiet reminders that happen every day when people drop their masks and reveal their hearts. This river of kindness flows through each and every one of us, connecting us.

Because kindness is more than just medicine. The act of giving and receiving is where the real magic of human connection occurs. It happens when people move past

14

the monotonous bullshit of what we do for work or how we feel about the weather, and into our private interior worlds — or as some people call them, our souls — to connect with one another and to heal. And I wanted more of it. Much, much more. What I discovered on my previous walk across America was that there is a rare and magnificent magic that happens when a stranger walks into town. Humans want to know about each other. They want to connect. So I figured what better way to find that magic again than by embarking on a mission of kindness around the world?

I stood there on Hollywood Boulevard and began to cry. Like, really cry. The kind of crying men don't do, at least not in the middle of the day on a busy street. They were old tears. Tears from growing up in a world where the people around me were often more interested in keeping a stiff upper lip than in genuinely connecting with the people around them, including me. And the only way to heal from that, the only way for all of us to heal, is through other people. It all made sense in that moment. I approached the homeless man with his serendipitous sign and put two $20 bills into his decrepit hat. That one act of *giving* was able to make me feel what I hadn't felt in years:

communion with another. Sure, I felt connected to the people in my life — my girlfriend, my family, the people I worked with — but what I was missing was that deep and impenetrable feeling that I was *one with* someone else. The man on the street smiled at me. I smiled in return. Then I rushed home, knowing exactly what I had to do.

And by "rushed home," I really mean "crawled along in a Los Angeles–size traffic jam." But that's the upside of traffic: it gives you time to think. It was then that I formulated my plan. I realized that my first foray across America had been all about *receiving* kindness (by travelling on only $5 a day), but for my next journey receiving was not going to be enough. This time I needed things to go full circle — I needed to *offer* kindness, as well as receive it.

By the time I emerged from traffic hell, I had already decided that I would circumnavigate the globe and that I would do it on a vintage motorbike. Like Che. The bike had to have a sidecar because you never knew who would need a helping hand. And it had to be yellow. Yes, yellow. Because yellow motorbikes are way cooler. I would have no money. No food. No place to stay. And the unnerving part — no gas. I also decided right away that I would not accept money. People could offer me food and lodging, but they could not give me the cash to pay for it myself. I wasn't looking for a free ride; I was looking for a shared one.

It dawned on me that I might be in the process of creating the first vehicle powered solely by kindness. Just as asking for help had allowed me to connect the last time I traveled across America, I figured it would do the same this time. "Why change a winning formula?" I wondered to myself.

But on this journey, I wouldn't just be asking for help. I would ultimately be offering something in return. Something life-changing. I wanted to reconnect to the world and hopefully, in some small way, reconnect my brothers and sisters of the world to themselves and to each other. I would use my own money to repay the kindness of those who had helped me. No one would be aware of my intentions beforehand. I didn't want people to know that if they showed me a random act of kindness they would receive anything in return. That's not the way it works. We don't give to get. We give to give. I couldn't help everyone who was kind and loving, but I would help as many as I could. And I would do so in life-changing, "Whoa, did that just

17

happen?" ways.

I made it home and ran up the steps to my house, taking them three at a time. I rushed into the living room to see my girlfriend sitting on the couch with her computer. Lina smiled at me from across the room, and as it often did in her presence, my heart relaxed a little.

I went toward her, and without even realizing it, I found myself bending down on one knee in front of her, "Babe," I began. "I need to tell you something."

I could see a flicker of joy in her eyes, and then I realized Lina was expecting a far grander proposal. For the last couple of months (ever since we had moved in together), she had begun to hint in increasingly stronger nudges that she wanted something akin to a promise from me. A promise that this was heading to commitment, heading toward children, heading toward the kind of life where she and I would be together, forever.

For. Ever.

Realizing that a bended knee was probably not the right gesture, I quickly stood up and announced, "I am going on a journey."

"Great," she said, her blonde hair falling loosely around her face as she looked back at her computer, hiding the swift disappointment I had seen cloud her eyes. "Where you off to?"

"Los Angeles."

"We're in Los Angeles, silly?" she laughed. "Are you going to the grocery store?"

Here goes, I thought to myself. It was now or never, "Not exactly, I'm going from Los Angeles to Los Angeles. I am going to circumnavigate the globe on a vintage yellow motorcycle."

Silence.

More silence.

"Babe," I began, a little concerned for my safety.

The laptop snapped closed, and she was back to life, "Are you serious?" Her face began to darken as she pleaded. "Leon, please tell me this is just another one of your wacky ideas."

Well, it certainly was wacky.

I hesitated. Did I really want to risk my relationship, my career . . . for kindness?

"I am deadly serious."

Then the crying began. And it didn't stop.

"Babe, I need to do this," I explained, the passion that had been missing from my life suddenly returned. I felt like Che driving out of that final scene and into the journey that would forever change his life, and many others. It wasn't just about seeing the world anymore; it was about bathing in its river.

"Why," she cried. "Haven't you already done enough existential cliff diving?"

"Yes, but the last time, I did it for me."

I stopped myself. I don't think I had quite realized it yet, but I didn't want this trip to be about me. Honestly, I had had enough of me. I wanted it to be a part of something so much bigger, something so much more important. I wanted it to be about you. Yes, *you*.

About all of us.

As I stood there trying to explain to the girlfriend who had just moved in why I now needed to leave, I actually thought that I no longer needed a revolution in *my* life. Instead, I yearned to create the ripples of Che's revolutionary spirit in others. It was about offering people the type of gift that wouldn't just change them, but transform them in the way that only kindness can. And through that transformation they would pass the torch to another, lighting the world through our connections. "My trip is just that first spark," I tried to explain to Lina.

She didn't reply at first, which was concerning. I honestly don't think there is a crueler punishment on earth than silence. But finally she looked up at me, and asked

20

the question I had tried so diligently not to ask myself: "Oh Leon, will you ever be able to stop running?"

I had no answer for her.

After about an hour of tears and recriminations, I managed to persuade her that although I was going to be away for up to six months, it would fly by quickly. She could see in my eyes and by this time, *my* tears, that I felt destined to take this journey. I knew my feet were taking me there. It wasn't a choice anymore.

"Just tell me this," Lina finally asked, wiping away her tears, "Do you think you can ever be happy . . . here?"

"Of course," I replied with as much honesty as I could muster.

Lina looked at me and sighed, "Look, I am proud of you for wanting to change the world, Leon. I just hope next time you can do it closer to home."

Change the world? Apparently, Lina had very high expectations.

Before this big adventure could happen, however, I had to deal with logistics, the great hurdle to any worthwhile dream. I needed to find a motorbike that would survive the rough roads and tough times that the journey would surely entail. I decided I would call it Kindness One, because, much like Air Force One, it would be an ambassador to the world . . . only a little yellower. I had to settle on an outline for my route around the globe. I also had to find a way to cross two oceans, a number of continents, a laundry list of cities, and a few hostile states on kindness alone, all with my yellow bike tagging along. And I needed to get visas, lots of them.

Then there was the little detail of *how* I wanted to do this. Would I bring along a TV crew to catalog my experiences, or would I be documenting my own adventure? I wanted the journey to be as intimate as possible, yet I also recognized how many people could potentially be touched by it through the medium of TV. I decided to go with the TV crew. But only under one condition: They would stay back until I invited them into whatever story or life I was joining. I wanted to do this trip alone. And I wanted to connect with people first before cameras showed up in the background. The crew would be the silent sidekicks of my adventure; but in many ways, they would also be my witnesses. As will you.

By the time this journey is over, I hope you will see how an act of kindness *really can* change the world. You will meet Tony,

22

the homeless man who taught me that true riches don't reside in our wallets but in our hearts. You will see the courage shown by my friend in Cambodia, whose life was ravaged by illness, loss, and natural disaster. You will meet a doctor whose passion for service restores the sight of the poor. You will see how one well-intentioned, but flawed human being can travel around the globe on the kindness of others and be reborn. And there are many others whom you will *not* meet: strangers who for a moment became friends, passing quickly through the day to offer me food, gas, and the means to keep going.

Salman Rushdie once wrote, "To understand just one life, you have to swallow the world." We don't have to travel this entire blue planet of ours to have that experience. We just have to be willing to *see* each other. I see you, and you see me. Then the masks of who we think we should be fall away. And we greet one another in ways that need no language, that require no masks. We set out on the journey of life, getting to partake in this brief but beautiful adventure together.

CHAPTER ONE

"You block your dream when you allow
your fear to grow bigger than your faith."
— Mary Manin Morrissey

There's always that moment before the big
moment. Those last sixty seconds before an
actor steps out on stage when he forgets his
lines, sweat breaking through his costume,
and he wonders why he ever thought this
was a good idea in the first place. But then
he steps out, and he knows in the very core
of his being: *this* is what he was meant to
do.

The night before I left, I wondered
whether leaving LA was such a good idea
after all. Work, relationships, routine — they
have their trappings as much as they can
make one feel trapped.

"So don't go," Lina suggested casually,
but I could hear the tightness in her voice
even as she tried to play it cool. That's one

of the downsides of loving someone: You always know what they're thinking. Or at least you think you do.

It might have seemed like a nonchalant enough suggestion, but in it, I heard, "Marry me now, or I will leave you forever."

It's no wonder I failed as a mind reader. Because though Lina didn't want me to go, she believed in my dreams. I just couldn't see that yet. What followed Lina's suggestion was what most people in relationships call a fight — although I prefer "minor disagreement." By the time we went to bed, we had attempted to make up, but all I could think was, "Tomorrow, it will just be me and Kindness One."

The next morning I could hear Lina in the kitchen as I got dressed. My dog, Winston, chased me around the house as I packed the final contents into my small black bag: a computer, a couple of changes of clothes, and some motorbike tools. In the back pocket of my bag, I tucked a postcard I had picked up on my previous journey across America. It read, "Life begins at the end of your comfort zone." Other than a bright yellow gas canister, that was all the luggage I would be bringing with me.

I had a globe to cross and a motorbike to ride, which sat outside my house, taunting me with my lack of mechanic skills.

I had bought the bike in Vegas only two weeks earlier. Unfortunately, it hadn't made it all the way home without incident. In Pasadena, only thirty miles from my house, the bike had revolted, breaking down on one of the busiest freeways in America. That's right, you heard me. On my first day of riding the damn thing, it couldn't even make it to LA from Vegas — and this was the bike I was trusting to get me around the world. I had to pay $450 just for it to be towed from Pasadena to Los Angeles. I wouldn't have $450 out there on the road. I wouldn't even have one dollar.

But perhaps even more troubling was the knowledge that though Kindness One looked good (and even had a new engine), the rest of it was built in 1978. Probably one of the only guarantees on this trip was that the bike *would* break down. I had taken a two-hour class on motorcycle maintenance, but failed to get any of the Zen. I bought the book, as the instructor suggested, but never got around to reading it. Sadly, the class didn't help too much, either.

On top of worrying about the bike malfunctioning, I was still not confirmed on a ship to cross the Atlantic (and I couldn't even begin to think about the Pacific crossing). Every day I made phone calls to shipping companies across the world. I had been put on hold for hours; I had begged people in foreign languages; I had friends begging people in foreign languages; I had cajoled, and once, just a little bit, for like a second, I had cried.

And then I spoke to Robert, who worked at a shipping company based overseas. He didn't tell me that I had safe passage, but he told me the next-best word to yes — *maybe.*

"You mean if I call you in two weeks, I might be able to get on a ship?" I asked.

"Yeah, it would be on a ship going from New York to Tarragona, Spain. . . . Maybe," Robert repeated the word as though I hadn't heard him the first time.

Lina opened the door to the bedroom and stood for a moment in the doorway. The sunlight hit her face and bounced off her blonde hair like a halo. I could tell she had been crying.

We both said the words at the same time, "I'm sorry."

I grabbed her tight, and whispered, "Don't worry. I'll be home soon."

I could feel her as she nodded into my shoulder, and I felt bad for conjuring up yet another adventure right after we had moved in together. I knew Lina had been hoping for one that centered more on wedding bells than yellow motorbikes. Finally, we let go of one another as she looked around the room, and said, "Well, I guess it's almost time."

Now, it was my turn to nod. What else could I say? I was leaving for six months, and as she walked out and back downstairs, I could only hope that she would still be there when I returned. Because part of me wanted to say yes to that adventure with her. The only problem was that every time I was home, I couldn't help but dream of where I might go next.

But before I went anywhere, I needed to find a tank of gas. I knew gas would probably be my greatest challenge. Food and water are actually easier to come by than most people realize, and if worst came to worst, I could always sleep in the sidecar of Kindness One, but the one thing that could definitely stall my journey on any given day, in any given location, was a lack of gas.

Lina might have called it running, but as I stepped outside my house and onto the street, the energy that coursed through me spoke to a far different word: freedom. The freedom of not knowing what lay ahead, whom I might meet, whom I might help, and the shocking realization that this truly outlandish idea was about to become reality.

I headed to Hollywood Boulevard, not far from where I had first seen the homeless man who had inspired the light-bulb moment in the first place, but he was nowhere to be found. Instead, I found far less generous people. Maybe they had just never seen the sign, "Kindness is the best medicine."

The first people I approached were two young men sporting fedora hats and what looked like their sister's jeans.

"Dude," the taller of the two admonished me, "You need to stop dreaming. Go home. You're wasting my time *and* your time."

Really, *dude*? You're wearing a fedora hat in the middle of summer. But I moved on, finding a young couple, walking with two Louis Vuitton shopping bags in hand. There you go, I thought, they've already opened their wallets today — and it looked like some pretty sizable wallets. Maybe they will open them to me.

"Sorry," they replied, assuming I was begging for money, which at this point, I kind of was. "We don't have anything."

Sadly, I too have made the same reply to a homeless person on the street, refusing to help when I knew that I could.

The next guy I asked appeared to be a

tourist, or at least I hoped he was, as he was in the middle of paying Iron Man for a photo. Not the real Iron Man, just one of the many struggling actors who dress up in character and roam Hollywood Boulevard. Once the photo op was done, I explained my journey.

He just shook his head at me like a disappointed father, "Stop mooching off the land, bro!"

Okay, then. Now I knew why I had been doubting myself the night before. I felt like a fool. I was walking around Hollywood Boulevard with a bright yellow gas canister, telling people about my journey, and they were ridiculing me. This wasn't in the script. Or at least not in the one I had written.

I left the jungle that is Hollywood Boulevard and decided that I might have better luck at a nearby gas station. I sat down on a bus-stop bench in front of the closest one, and tried to relax. And by relax, I mean I sat down to question how was I ever going to make it across the world when I couldn't even make it out of Los Angeles. Was Lina right? Was this whole scheme just another means of escape?

Years before I met Lina, I dated a beautiful, smart, sophisticated, and kind woman named Michelle. I was lucky in fact to have found all those same qualities in Lina. But the comparison didn't end there. Michelle and I were together for five years. We lived together. We made dinner together. We adopted a dog together. But the one thing we didn't do — or rather, the one thing *I* couldn't do — was get married.

After five years, Michelle had had enough. She threatened to leave. I managed to convince her that before we threw it all away, maybe we should see a therapist, someone who, I thought, would naturally see my side, explaining to Michelle why being married is no guarantee of commitment.

By the end of our fourth session, Michelle and I were refusing to speak to one another, and the therapist was tired of talking. She sat back and suggested we do some more work on our own before we came back to her office.

"Are you breaking up with us?" I asked her.

"No," the therapist nervously laughed, "I just don't think you're ready to do the work that this takes. Getting married isn't just about a wedding. It's about creating a connection that can withstand whatever life might throw at it. That takes a lot of commitment. It takes a lot of effort. It takes patience."

As I sat on that bench, I wondered if I was simply being impatient. Something doesn't work out in my life, so I find something else. I don't stick around to fix it; I just replace it. I wondered if this trip was quickly going the same way. Would I have the patience to wait for kindness?

I looked up to see a man walking toward me. That man was Dwight. I will say it here, right now, to make it official: Dwight was my first angel. Resembling a young Jamie Foxx, with his cool mirrored sunglasses and a white towel inexplicably thrown over one shoulder like a boxing coach (which in many ways he was for me), Dwight noticed me sitting on the bus-stop bench and nodded in my direction.

That was enough interaction for me. I jumped up and hastily explained my adventure: "I'm driving across the world, on a yellow motorbike, basically, well, on the kindness of strangers. This is my gas can. I need gas. But I won't even be able to leave my house if I don't get this first tank of gas."

I'm sure that elevator speech would have gotten me an "F" in any Marketing 101 class, but it caught Dwight's attention. "You are traveling around the world on kindness? On a yellow motorbike? Really?" he asked, repeating my story.

"Really," I confirmed.

"*Really,* really?"

"Yes, I know it sounds nuts, but I am, and I need help." And then I waited.

"All right," he said with a shrug.

I jumped and hugged him, nearly knocking us both off balance.

"I could kiss you," I cried.

"Please don't," Dwight laughed as we walked to the pump with my empty gas canister. The irony was Dwight was not even getting gas. He didn't even have a car. But what he did have was a dream. I found out that Dwight had once worked as a truck driver, driving all over the country, but never had the chance to stop and get to know the cities and towns that dotted his route.

"Man," he enthused. "I just wish I was doing something like you. I always wanted to just get out there, you know. Just take off, travel, see the world."

"Why don't you?" I asked, although I already knew the answer. For so many, finances trap us in worlds we can't escape and deny us worlds we might never get the chance to know.

"It's just hard, you know," he explained. "You have to work to travel and then you can't travel because you have to work."

34

Dwight shrugged the statement off as though it didn't mean anything to him, but I could see his mask drop for a moment, just long enough to see the yearning pass quickly across his eyes — a desire for the freedom that I was about to experience, especially now that I had my first tank of gas.

I took down Dwight's details so I could share with him my trip across the world. It was why I had brought along the computer — to blog for anyone who wanted to listen, and to keep Lina and my friends and family up to date, but also to connect with all the new friends I met along the way.

After Kindness One and I left our street, it took about 45 minutes to work my way through LA traffic before the road opened up and I found my stride. I thought of Dwight as I rode, wishing that one day he would feel this exhilaration, the feeling that every cell in his body was electrified with hope. Sure, I was once again leaving behind my life and taking off into the sunset, and sure this was a totally insane idea with totally crazy possibilities, but as the sun reflected off the desert sands around me and I watched two hawks fly up ahead of me, the world had never looked more perfect.

I pulled over in The Mojave Desert, almost halfway to Vegas, as my gas tank was running low. There, I found another Good Samaritan, who filled me up in the scorching heat. Back on the road we went, and before I knew it, I was standing next to the world-famous Las Vegas sign. Welcome to Vegas, indeed.

I engaged in my first sinful act by parking the bike illegally, praying there were no parking enforcement officers on the prowl. I guess you can't go to Vegas and be completely sin free. The first person I approached, seeking a place to stay for the night, was Gene Simmons. Okay, maybe not *the* Gene Simmons but a rather impressive lookalike. I thought for sure such a renowned man of the bedroom might have one to spare. I was wrong. I was also wrong about the three masked Mexican wrestlers. The afternoon was drawing to a close, and I was getting desperate.

I walked down Fremont Street, where Vegas locals were rumored to hang out. I found myself in a large outdoor shopping promenade, looking through the mass of people wandering by me in search of one that stood out. And then I saw him. I wasn't sure if it was the elaborate moustache or the bright orange vest, but this guy screamed, "Talk to me!"

I took in a deep breath and felt another part of myself emerge — the court jester, the class clown, the boy who discovered that as long as he could make people laugh, he could also make them like him a little. It was a mask, but that's the thing with masks: They can serve a purpose.

"My friend, that is quite a moustache. Is it real?" I asked, hoping my interest would spark a conversation.

"Of course it's real," he smiled.

"Really," I feigned doubt. "Can I touch it?"

Thankfully, my new friend didn't get totally unnerved by the request. He laughed, telling me, "Well, normally, only ladies are allowed to do that, but you can, real quick."

Since this man was open enough to let me touch his face in the first few minutes of our exchange, I thought he might also be the kind of person who would appreciate a good story. After telling him only a bit of mine, he interrupted me with a hearty laugh, "I also believe in the kindness of strangers." Maurice's moustache moved in perfect unison with his mouth, like two synchronized swimmers dancing in a pool. "In the end only kindness matters."

And then to my amazement he offered me

a place to stay.

"Are you sure?" I asked him, thrilled and shocked by his proposal.

"Sure, I'm sure," was his hearty reply.

Suddenly, that moment on the bench, that moment with Lina the previous night, that moment in the therapist's office years ago, all seemed eons away. This was the adventure I was supposed to be on. Just as I had found gas in LA, I had found a place to stay in Las Vegas, kindness reminding me that everything was going according to plan. Maurice suggested I come to his house at 8:30 p.m. He gave me an improvised map before I headed back to Kindness One with a few hours to kill.

I walked around Vegas just as the temperature began to cool, coming down to a gentle 100 degrees. I watched a young skateboarder pull up to a kebab stand. Wait a second, kebab stand? All I had eaten that day was Lina's breakfast. I walked up to the young chap hoping he would help. Though I had had terrible luck with twenty-something hipsters in Hollywood, I hoped their Vegas counterparts would be kinder. And sure enough, Vegas Hipsters: 1, Hollywood Hipsters: 0.

Richard was impressed with my journey around the world.

"Man," he grunted, staring off into the approaching sunset of the Vegas sky, "I would love to do something like that."

"Really?" I asked.

"Yeah, I mean, I'm trying to go pro," he nodded down at the skateboard by his feet, "so I hope, you know, one day I might tour and shit."

"Where would you like to go?"

"I don't know," Richard shrugged. "I never been out of Nevada, so anywhere I guess. Mexico, Jamaica. Where are you going?"

It was a hard question. I knew I was ultimately heading back to Los Angeles, I had secured visas in a number of countries, but I didn't have much more of a concrete plan than that.

"I know I have to go to New York," I told him. "That's how I'm planning to get overseas."

"Oh wow. It would be so cool to go to New York."

He looked back down at his skateboard, kicking it back up into his hand, "But I'll probably just end up staying here."

As I finished the kebab Richard had just bought me, I hoped that one day he would learn that you won't go anywhere unless you believe in yourself. Unless you're willing to do the work — to make the commitment, to put in the effort, to have the patience — you'll end up stuck in the same place. Maybe that therapist was right. It wasn't about a wedding. It was about what it takes to live your dream.

But I knew what it was like to be young and lost — to live with wanderlust and not be able to make the right decisions to indulge it. The world is filled with people who dream of being Hemingway, but more often settle for far less. And it's not their fault. We have bills to pay and children to raise and parents to look after — and we lose sight of the quiet burning dream inside that craved something more. It was that dream that had forced me out of bed just hours before, and would push me along on the much more difficult days to come.

We finished our kebabs, and Richard walked me to Kindness One to see the infamous yellow motorbike in the flesh. I offered him a ride in the sidecar, and then it happened. The bike broke down. Again. On the first day. Richard helped me push it to the side of the road, but he could see that I was not in a good state.

"Yo, dude, your bike doesn't look too well," he offered.

No shit dude, I thought to myself.

40

As a puff of smoke leapt out of the engine, Richard gave me that universal look that says, "Well, I wish I could help you, but you're kind of on your own. . . ."

To make matters worse it was now 8:18 p.m., and I was in danger of losing my place to stay for the night. For a moment, my outsides were calm, but then like a volcano bubbling up from below, my anxious insides began to pour out, and I had what they call in England a "wobbly," or as Americans might know it, a meltdown.

"This can't be happening!" I yelled, surprising Richard and myself with my outburst. "My first day, my first day!"

Sure, people stopped and looked. Sure, I kicked the curb a couple of times (or twelve). But I didn't care. What on earth could be wrong with my bike? I was screwed. The bike wouldn't start, and my hopes of staying somewhere for the night were fast receding with the Nevada sun.

Finally, I stopped yelling and remembered what the mechanic had told me in LA: "Remember, never ride the bike with the petcock switched off. Never!" I don't expect that you know what a petcock is, but if you do, then you would know that petcocks are never to be turned off when riding. Never! I switched the pesky little petcock *on* and

41

started the engine.

I had to rush to the house of the biggest mustache in Nevada, thanking Richard and all the passers-by who had witnessed my small moment of indiscipline. From my rearview mirror, I could see Richard watching me as I left, and I hoped that one day he would be the one riding off into the sunset.

Though most of the other houses on Maurice's suburban street were lit up, his was pitch black, making it look like no one was home. My worst fears were realized. I had arrived 45 minutes late, and Maurice had gone to sleep. Maybe he had come to his senses and decided that inviting a random Englishman into his home wasn't such a good idea after all.

I kept manically pressing the doorbell and considered jumping over the gate, but then I remembered this was America and most people have guns, particularly people with big moustaches (that's my last joke, I promise). I couldn't help but wonder what I was doing all this for. I mean, I wanted to show that the world could be kind, I wanted to be a part of its kindness, but was this really the only way I could do it? Did I always have to leave home in order to prove a point? And just what was I trying to prove, anyway? That strange men with large moustaches would open their homes to even stranger men with yellow motorbikes? Did I really need to cross the world to find that out?

"We didn't know if you were going to make it," Maurice called out just as I began to walk away.

Maurice was approaching his gate as I told him, "I almost didn't."

"Come on in, son," he replied as we went into his house. The house was filled with people and animals and far too many details for my weary brain to keep track of. All I knew was that my first day across the world was going to end with a bed.

The next two days were spent riding farther east across the vastness of America. Kindness One was quickly becoming somewhat of a celebrity, with locals across the country buying me gas, offering me bottles of water, a quick lunch, or a kind smile before going on their way.

It seems like every day we are inundated with heartbreaking stories of war, cancer, and death. It can become easy to believe that people only know how to treat each other badly. But I don't believe that's our true nature. The kindness that runs through us is what's genuine. It's built into the smallest gestures — a "Best wishes!" or an "All right, mate!" called out from a stranger — and in the big ones, the ones that take everyone right out of their comfort zone, uniting them through love or compassion or just two strangers dropping their masks and connecting with each other for a remarkable moment.

As I drove out of Utah and into Colorado, I looked up to find a double rainbow stretching across the towering Rocky Mountain skyline. Maybe because I slightly feared what was ahead, all I could do was appreciate the present moment. I had no iPhone to distract me. No Internet to take me away from my Zen. In that moment, surrounded by nature's extreme beauty, I realized that in this time of endless calls and texts and Insta-everything, we think we are connected. But it's a false connectivity. What we often lose is that relationship with the deeper fiber of life. As I drove through the crisp Rockies, the summer morning expanding before me, I knew that this was the real network. This was connection.

And that's when I saw the old English taxicab, serendipity once again gently touching me on my shoulder. What are the odds of seeing an English cab in the middle of rural Colorado? I will tell you, about infinity to one.

I drove into the nearest town, and found myself at the Chamber of Commerce. There I discovered that not only was I probably in the only town in Colorado with an English cab, but I was also probably in the only town in Colorado with a Scotsman. The lady at the Chamber of Commerce put me on the phone with Willy, who the woman clearly hoped would help me because we both had strange accents. She was right.

Within a few minutes of conversation, Willy agreed to put me up for the night. I thanked the ladies at the Chamber of Commerce and drove off to Willy's house. And I almost made it there too, but then my left side mirror fell off. You know, the one that tells me whether there's a car driving on my left side.

Here I was on day two, and the bike was already starting to fall apart.

Lina had asked me what would happen if the bike died, and I'd had no reply. I could still remember hers.

"Are you just never going to come home?"

"What, don't be ridiculous," was my insensitive reply. Yet the question still lingered: Would I ever make it back?

I guess my mirror was going to have to be

broken for a while. A long while as it turned out. I put it in my backpack and drove on.

As soon as I arrived at Willy's home, with its white shutters and flower-lined path leading up to his front door, I felt at ease. The long drive, the stress of finding a bed, the fear that I might run out of gas and not find anyone willing to help me, it all faded as Willy invited me into his backyard, which was filled with an herb garden, roses, and a small waterfall that trickled into a pond.

As we sat talking, Willy explained that he had been living in Colorado for years. Then he had what I soon realized was a natural response to my own journey: He dropped his mask and shared his life story with me.

Willy grew up in the coal mines of Scotland. He worked there for eleven years before finally getting out of those dark and miserable tunnels. His cousin lost an arm in them, and he had once seen a man killed. When he left his home for America, he dreamed of a different life.

As he gestured to his tranquil backyard, he said, "I dreamt of this."

But Willy imagined more than his yard, he dreamed of helping people.

He sat back in his chair as he explained, "You know, we get the chance to be a lot of people in life. For me, everything changed in 1984. . . ."

He paused before explaining, "You see, I went to hear Billy Graham speak, you know the famous pastor."

"Sure," I said, having heard of Billy Graham long before coming to America.

"I guess, before that day, I had always felt a bit lost. I mean, I would go to work, I raised my children, but I wasn't really living the life I thought I should be. Does that make sense?"

I nodded. Some people call it a rut. I call it one of life's greatest tragedies. But Willy had found his way out of that rut just as surely as he had found his way out of the mines.

Willy continued, "After I heard Reverend Graham, I just, well, I had this feeling like I knew why I was sent here. I was here to help people."

I found out that after that day, he started working with the homeless, and then he found himself at a suicide hotline. And now he worked with the elderly. He smiled softly as he shared with me, "My mother used to say, 'We all can find ourselves disconnected from love.' "

We can. And sometimes all it takes is that friendly Scottish voice on the other end of the line or sitting across from us to make us feel connected again. He told me how his sons now lived in England, and we both talked about how hard it was to leave behind those we loved. I understood that longing. I had felt it as I went to bed on Maurice's futon the night before, only six hours away (at least that's how long the trip took on good old Kindness One) — and yet so far — from home. Though I had met many great people already on this journey, I realized that in Willy, I was meeting a friend.

Willy's wife, Chery soon came home, and he told me that it was the ninety-sixth birthday of one of his friends, Kay.

He smiled sadly, "If we don't bring her cake, I'm afraid no one else will."

As Chery bought a cake for Kay, my new Scottish friend told me how his son was getting married that summer. But as I soon found out, they were not going to be able to attend. The wedding was going to be in the UK, and Willy and Chery could not afford the price of the airline tickets.

Willy's mouth was smiling, but his eyes glistened with an unspoken pain as he said tightly, "Leave it to them to pick the most expensive time of year."

"You're not going to be able to go?" I asked, heartbroken for this kind man who could connect with so many strangers yet was not able to see the ones he loved most.

Willy didn't say anything at first but then admitted, "We just can't afford it."

He added with a touch of Scottish pride, "Besides folks need us here."

I saw the sadness wash over his face. He looked at Chery, who gave him a reassuring look, a look that spoke a thousand words. *All will be okay, my love.*

I wondered if next to Billy Graham, the other most important moment in Willy's life had been when he met Chery. I knew that is what I had with Lina — the meaningful glance, the loving support, the "I got you babe" that we rarely ever get elsewhere in life.

I left Kindness One in Willy's garage and rode to Kay's in the back of his pickup truck. Willy let us into Kay's house. She sat in the twilight of the afternoon without any lights on, the light of the television reflecting on her face, and then she turned, and the whole room lit up.

Everyone in the world should know a woman like Kay. At ninety-six years old, she had more energy than most people half her age. She giggled at all my jokes and kept thanking Willy and Chery for the cake. Even though we were her first birthday guests, she didn't seem to care — she was just happy that Willy was there.

She curled into her armchair, clutching a heavy blanket to her body, and told me, "Getting old is for the young!"

She laughed at her little joke before getting more serious, "It's true, though. You get old and suddenly everyone you know is gone, and you realize that, well, it just doesn't last long enough."

Willy laughed, "Well, Kay, we hope we can all make it to ninety-six."

She winked at him, "That's why I love this man. He makes me feel like I'm part of the human race. And not just some old leftover luggage."

She laughed softly, reminding me of how often we toss our elders aside, forgetting to love them when they need us most. Like Willy said, people found themselves disconnected from love. And that's what he returned to Kay.

As I was leaving I kissed Kay on the cheek.

She giggled at the gesture, "I can give you the other cheek too."

Laughter filled the house and followed me as I sat in the back of Willy's truck, while he drove us back to his house for the night. As a cool summer night passed by me, I began to think about the gifts I wanted to give. Sure, I had mapped out as much of my journey as I could, had gotten my visas, was working on my transatlantic passage, but the one thing I hadn't sorted out was whom I was going to give these gifts to. And what were the gifts supposed to be, anyway? I had been waiting the last two days for inspiration to strike, and then suddenly, sitting in the back of Willy's truck, inspiration came sailing in, or rather soared above me. A plane.

Yes, a plane. That is what I could give Willy. I could give him and Chery a trip to attend their son's wedding. I could send them home. But more than anything, I could answer their unfulfilled dream — the one thing they wanted so badly, they were afraid to admit they even wanted it at all.

That was the trick. It was getting to know people on such a level, connecting with them in such a way that instead of thinking about me, I would pay attention to them, which might very well be the deepest connection of all. I would try to hear, between their words, what really mattered most to them. I wanted to give them a gift that would fulfill the dreams they kept silent. And I wanted to learn to listen closely enough so that I could hear it.

After we all got home, we sat down in their living room. I felt very much at home.

Though there would be many strange nights in my future, where I would slip awkwardly off to bed and try not to wake anyone when I left in the morning, that wasn't the case with Willy.

"It must be difficult being so far away from your sons," I began, gearing up for my big surprise.

"Yeah it's been quite a while since I've seen them," Willy told me wistfully.

Chery interrupted, clearly knowing what Willy wouldn't say, "Oh, he misses them every day. No matter how old they are, you always feel like a part of you is missing when they're gone."

I nodded, "Well, that's actually why I wanted to talk with you. Because, well, first of all I want to thank you both for letting me stay in your house, introducing me to Kay. It's all been an amazing act of kindness."

They smiled at me, unsure of how to respond.

I forged ahead, explaining, "But for me it's not just about the kindness you've shown me, it's about the kindness that clearly lives everywhere in your life. With your families and each other and the people you help. I know you've given something to me without expecting anything in return. It seems that's just the way you live your life. Which is very rare. But I'd like to offer you something in return."

I paused for a moment as I prepared to tell them, "I want to pay for you to go to your son's wedding."

After years of offering a sense of family to those who were disconnected from their own, it was time for Willy to see his real family. Willy's face went white, and I could see as the tears filled his eyes, that this was that one thing, that special little dream that we all keep alive even when we don't know how we're going to make it happen. After a moment of stunned silence all he could say was, "You're joking?"

"I am absolutely not joking," I replied.

"You're serious?" Willy asked with a straight poker face.

"I am very serious."

His mouth began to quiver, this strong man finally letting go of his Scottish pride to accept that generosity can go both ways. It always should.

"I'm speechless," Willy finally replied, a smile breaking across his face. "An English-man has made me speechless!"

"And that's the first time a Scotsman's ever been speechless," I teased back.

"This is the answer to my prayers," Willy

quietly whispered, the tears beginning to flow. He gave me a big hug, and this time it was someone else who wouldn't let go. I could feel his body shaking as the emotions overtook him. This big-hearted man was finally dropping his own mask. The one that pretended that he was okay with not seeing his son get married, the one that acted as if being of service to others could somehow replace the love he felt for his family. He finally pulled away and said, "This is what faith brings."

I excused myself and went to my room to go to sleep. I pulled out my computer before going to bed and sent out an email. It was short and sweet, a little shot in the dark to the home I had left behind. It was to Lina, and it said the three most important words one human being can say to another, "I love you."

CHAPTER TWO

"All for one and one for all."
— Alexandre Dumas

I don't remember if it was just one particular Monday or a series of Mondays that led to the rock bottom of my life in London. All I do remember is that I was sitting there, in my oak-wood office, with my oak-wood desk. Metal bookcases spanned across one wall, and on the other hung an antique hunting painting you would expect to find in an old law office. The white walls stood out in stark contrast against the gray skies of London just beyond my windows. I blinked hard at the flashing cursor on my computer and reached out to pick up the ringing phone. And I wanted everything to change. Literally, everything.

Sure, I worked in Mayfair, the Beverly Hills of London. And sure, I made money, but to me, it was all meaningless. Because for years, I thought that if I could only make more, if I could only achieve more, that somehow I would *be* more. More of what, I had no idea. Because no matter how many zeroes I put in my bank account, I always felt bankrupt inside.

After landing in Los Angeles I worked hard to eradicate that part of my life. I traveled. I spent time connecting with people, and spent as little time in an office as possible. But then slowly, things began to change.

I started working on a new project in the TV business. My days in the office got longer; my nights at home got shorter. If I wasn't at work, I was thinking about work. I lived on my laptop, and when not on my laptop, I lived on my phone. I thought for sure if I could just get this one TV show off the ground, everything would be right with the world. I had replaced one superficial gig for another, but I couldn't see that. Instead, I simply believed I was following a dream. I was making things happen. And I was becoming an annoying coworker, friend, and partner in the process.

Lina would ask me to do something on the weekend, and I would invariably be an hour late. She would be upset, but I would explain, "Babe, this project is about to happen. I swear. And then it will all be over."

How right I was, because two weeks before I was supposed to leave for the new TV show I was producing, I got the call — the green light had turned red. The show was being canceled.

All the hours, all the hard work, all the angry voicemails from my girlfriend went down the drain, and my ego went down right there with it. I shut down entirely. I wouldn't talk to Lina about it. I wouldn't get out of bed. Lina would go to work, and I would draw the shades and hide.

Until one day, she came home and opened them for me, saying without words, "Enough." That was the day I went to Hollywood Boulevard, the day I saw the homeless man. And I knew, just as I knew on that rainy Monday in London, that change doesn't come to us. We must go seek it.

After three days of driving through the golden haze of America's heartland — through sun-drenched wheat fields and mind-blowing sunsets, I finally arrived at the outskirts of the sleepy city of Lexington, Nebraska. One aspect of Nebraska I wasn't prepared for were all the bloody cornfields. Lots and lots of cornfields. So many that I lost count after the first 116.

I pulled off the highway and found myself on an old farm road. This was the America I had often imagined, without even realizing that it actually existed: endless farmland with big red barns, tall water towers, and grain silos dotting an otherwise flat landscape. I stopped to look around. In so many ways, this was exactly what I had left London for: the fresh air of an open land, the beauty of an unknown destination; and in many ways, it was also why I left LA. Because as much as I loved Lina and our life, I also loved this. I loved being free.

I got back on my bike, a lone wolf driving through the prairie, a stranger in a strange town, and a desperate chap who was about to run out of gas. But then again, I always ran out of gas. That's part of the deal when you're driving across the world with no money. But it was also the driving force of this adventure. Not knowing where this road might take me was taking me down wonderful, twisting, and unexpected roads. I pulled into the small town of Lexington, ready for whatever might happen next.

I saw the men almost immediately — they were in an obscenely large pickup truck, wore dusty hats, and one of them even had some tobacco in his mouth. That's right, cowboys.

"Excuse me," I asked the older one after he closed his truck door. "Very random question, but are you a cowboy?"

Without even blinking, he answered me matter-of-factly, "Yes."

Darrel was wearing a dark red cowboy shirt and cowboy jeans and a cowboy belt, and, oh my goodness, I couldn't help myself from exclaiming, "You even have cowboy shoes?!"

(Yes, I said that.)

Not my most polished introduction, I know. But it's been a long-standing dream of mine to be a cowboy, and if this trip was all about making people's dreams come true, I figured it didn't hurt if one of them was mine. I asked them if they had a farm, and when I found out they did, I offered my services in exchange for a place to sleep.

Darrel and his ranch hand, Seth, had just come into town to pick up some supplies. I figured if Seth could apprentice on the farm, why couldn't I? Darrel answered me just as calmly as before, as though he was asked this question every day, "Yeah, we can do that."

I followed them down the highway and onto one of the most picturesque roads I had ever seen; it felt like I was driving slap-bang into the middle of the movie *Field of*

Dreams.

The first thing Darrel did was introduce me to his family, all ten of them. They all seemed genuinely happy to meet me. Entertained by my fascination with all things cowboy, they were willing to indulge me, even dressing me up as one and taking me on a tour of the farm, led by an eight-year-old girl who drove me around in an ATV. I guess what happens in Nebraska stays in Nebraska, unless you meet some pesky Englishman who tells everyone your secrets.

I will tell you right now, lest you think I had some previous skills in this area: I have never lassoed anything before in my life. Ever. So when Darrel handed me a rope and asked me to lasso one of his cows, which was minding its own business in a nearby field, I felt a tinge of apprehension. I mean, a moving target? Sure it was a bloody slow-moving one, but still? Even worse than the challenge was the fear that I might fail and a make fool of myself in front of my new friends.

All my life, I have feared failure. Maybe that's why I decided it was easier to be the jester, everyone expects the jester to mess it all up. As I sent the rope forth only to watch it fall feet away from my intended target, I could feel the mask of silliness rise up and

60

envelop my very being. Suddenly, I didn't want to fail at this.

As Darrel walked up to take back the rope, I gently stopped him.

"No, please give me one more try." I breathed in deep, let go of the jester, and out soared the rope, falling beautifully across Bessie's neck. (She didn't actually have a name, so we'll just call her Bessie for posterity.)

Darrel and his grandsons cheered. I thought I surely earned their respect, their admiration, but only minutes later, as I was getting on a horse for the first time, I could hear Seth telling one of the kids, "He's like an eight-year-old cowboy, but he can learn."

After making fun of me for hours, Darrel and the rest of his family finally decided it was time to feed this bruised and humiliated Englishman some good ol' cowboy burgers. Cheeseburgers? Now that, I'm good at.

As the sun set in the distance, the mirrored sky fading across the fields, I thanked this amazing family for taking a day out of their life to show me theirs. We sat together in the quiet of the evening, and I realized this was the real upside of cowboy life — the small moments that filled their lives. The big stuff, the grand moments, will always come and go. But it's the little ones that have the real potential to change us.

I stayed that night with my cowboy friends and could feel the connection to life that their work brought them. When I was a boy, we would go and visit a small island in Greece called Chios, where my mother was from and where my grandmother still lives. Growing up in the city, I found it exhilarating to be on an island where we felt safe and could go and do whatever our little imaginations desired. We jumped off rocky cliffs and ran wild through the villages. But it wasn't just hanging out with my fellow little people with funny Greek accents that made me love those summers; it was the freedom of connecting with the land. For Darrel, his family, and Seth, every day brought that connection. I could feel it in them, and for the first time in a long time, I could feel it in me.

I left the farm the next morning and headed back to the big city — driving towards Chicago. My heart was filled with love. I spent an evening in Chicago and, after struggling through another breakdown with the bike, received some great news. The shipping company had sent an email confirming that I was all set for the ship to Europe! I would have to be in New York in a few days so the bike could be crated for its journey across the Atlantic Ocean. I was still 793 miles away from New York, though, and was suddenly in a race against time.

I headed east, straight through the heart of Amish country. I thought the Amish would be the easiest group to ask for help, but when I told a local shopkeeper about the camera crew waiting outside, he replied, "The local folks, they're going to have issues with those cameras."

That's right. My trusty team of producers, who hovered ever so silently in the background, went against one of the main testaments of the Amish: no graven images. However, cameras off, one Amish family helped me with a tank of gas, and I found a local pastor whose humble and gracious family were willing to house one exhausted and scruffy Brit for the night.

The next day, I got back into my same shabby outfit, had a small bite to eat, and breathed in the deep morning air. Small moments, indeed.

And then I got pulled over.

"You see, officer," I explained to the Pennsylvania state trooper, "I am on a mission of kindness. Me and my bike here, Kindness One. Kind of like Air Force One, the president's . . ."

He grunted, "Uh huh."

"Oh, okay. So though driving 52 in a 45 on a yellow motorbike might be technically illegal, I didn't mean to do it illegally."

I waited. I am sure he was deciding the chances of ever seeing this ticket paid by an Englishman on a bright yellow bike. He looked me up and down, and then let me off with a warning. The magic of yellowness, I say!

It was time to decide where to go to next, and I picked Pittsburgh. Because, well, why not? I drove to the center of town and parked near one of the local parks.

The only downside of parks in big cities is that as much as they might be a great place to meet people, they also often contain the sadder side of life — vagrants and homeless people — and, depending where you are, crime.

Before I even entered the park, however, I noticed an old food cart on the sidewalk, operated by an elderly white man. I found out that Gus had been shaving ice in the park for the last sixty-five years, watching as it went from a peaceful gathering space for the neighborhood to one mired in drugs and gang violence. I found out later, though, that all the gangs had formed a truce to protect Gus; no one was allowed to hurt him.

I regaled Gus with stories of my journey as he scraped up some shaved ice into a paper cone for me. As I enjoyed my afternoon treat, it was his turn to regale me, not with stories, but with wisdom. "Never give up, Leon. Sometimes in life, no matter what happens, we have to just keep going."

I headed off into the park only to find that many of the people inside were homeless, sitting next to large bundles of blankets and bags filled with their only belongings. I watched a man walk in from the street, and I felt compelled to talk with him. He was a stocky African-American man with an open, friendly face. He walked calmly towards me, as though he were just on an early evening stroll.

"Can I bore you with a story?" I began.

The man stopped and smiled, "Sure."

I gave him the song and dance that we all know by now: journey around the world, Kindness One, no money, no food, no gas, no place to stay for the night. And then I came to my punch line, "Can I live in your house tonight?"

Can I live in your house tonight! What are you thinking, man?

His response was not what I was expecting. He smiled softly at me as he explained, "Unfortunately I don't have a house. I'm homeless right now."

He continued, "But if I did, you'd be more than welcome there, as I've always opened my doors to strangers in the past. I live outside right now — in fact just a few feet from where we're standing, right over there."

He pointed to a small courtyard beyond the park. I didn't know what to say. I honestly hadn't expected his response. I found out his name was Tony, and to be honest, Tony didn't look homeless. He looked like a hard-working man walking home after a long day on the job.

I finally managed to reply, "You seem like someone with a very kind heart."

"So I've been told," he laughed. "I've always been kindhearted. I was raised that way."

He paused for a moment, before offering sheepishly, "If you need a place to stay though, you're more than welcome to stay with us."

I realized that he meant joining him and his friends on the streets. I'll admit — a part of me was afraid, and another part of me was concerned that I would be taking from people who had so little, but there was something about Tony's offer that made me feel like he really wanted to help. I sensed that he wanted the opportunity to give. And I was learning just how good that could feel.

I smiled, my hand falling upon my heart, "Well, if your friends are willing to have me, and you're willing to have me, then I would be grateful to stay with you."

"We'd appreciate that," he nodded as though he had been waiting all day for me to show up. "We'd enjoy it."

We walked over to his camp, where four other people were already hanging out, including Tony's good friend Richard. They seemed slightly surprised by my entrance, but as we sat down and began to chat, everyone started to relax into the time-old tradition of storytelling.

Tony shared how his life had brought him to the park. I don't know why some win in the lottery of fate while others are constantly dealt a rough hand, but Tony seemed to be a good man who had been through a bad life. After his father died when he was eight, his mother began drinking. Years of poverty and trauma, pain, and street life ensued. Tony had gotten himself into his fair share of trouble, but he had also tried time and time again to get himself out of it.

I looked around at the other men as they

nodded somberly at Tony's story. I knew that these tales were far too common. Lives that were forever set on the wrong course before the people involved could alter their own destinies. Their dreams had been dimmed so long ago that they barely remembered what they were in the first place.

Tony and I started talking about helping others. "Why did you help me today?" I asked. "I mean giving me a place to stay, inviting me here with your friends."

He shrugged his shoulders and replied, "It's just a way of giving back. That's my philosophy on life — giving is always good. Much better to give than receive. That's how I've always felt."

He laughed quietly, "Maybe that's why I'm poor."

Later, Tony would give me some of the new clean clothes he had received at a shelter because he was worried that I wouldn't have enough for my journey. I didn't know what to say then, and I'm still not too sure I know what to say now. The small moments, the small acts, they break the heart wide open.

As most of Tony's friends dispersed for the night, I couldn't quite believe that I was about to sleep on the streets of Pittsburgh. Gus, the wise ice shaver, had told me that this park was one of the most dangerous places in town, and I was sleeping on its sidewalk. But, for some reason, I felt safe with Tony. Like Willy in Colorado, I had met a friend, one I hoped to keep for a long time. Tony gave me some of the hamburgers another friend had given him for dinner, offering me what little food he had. As we ate, I wondered what Tony's dream had been. When he was a young boy, before his father died, before he found himself here in this park, what had he hoped to become?

We prepared our "beds," using cardboard and some old tattered blankets. Tony suggested that I sleep with my bag underneath my head so "it didn't walk off in the middle of the night." Amazingly, I managed to fall into a fitful sleep — that is, until I heard Richard screaming. You remember that part, right? The little incident at the beginning of this story that made me ask, "Why on earth am I doing this, again?"

Tony got up, and put his arm around his friend, which calmed him down. He offered him a place to sit on his makeshift bed, and Richard was able to shake off his fear of the strange man lurking in some other part of the park. Tony reassured me in the dark, "Don't worry. Stuff like that happens all the time." That really didn't make me feel better, but somehow I knew this man would look after me.

I know that sometimes home is just a temporary space, the small little nook we carve out between where we've been and where we're going, and in that place, we create family. We have no choice but to create family. In many ways, I felt more connected to Tony than I did to those I knew and loved. Suddenly, the big deal, the great project, whatever insignificant thing I thought was important faded away. In that moment, the only thing that mattered was my connection with this human being. In the morning, I found out just how right my instinct was.

"Did you get any sleep?" I asked as I folded up my bed.

"I slept okay. Just trying to keep those bugs off you."

Those bugs off me?

All throughout the night, while I snored dutifully away, Tony had been picking the bugs off of me, trying to keep me safe and comfortable.

Unlike being a cowboy, I have never dreamed of being homeless. I doubt anybody has. But I always had preconceived ideas about what it meant. Primarily that you had to be a drug addict or mentally ill.

I wanted to deny the idea that a good, honest man could find his way down the rabbit hole, just through poor luck and bad decisions.

The night before, Tony had told me how he had tried to go to school at least six different times over the years. When I asked what he had wanted to study, he laughed, "Anything that would give me a better life."

But then he stopped, truth rising up out of his easy reply, "I've always wanted to cook."

"Really?" I asked.

"Yeah, I don't know. I guess, I like taking care of people, and you know, the best way to do that is to fill their bellies." He chuckled.

As I tossed and turned throughout the night, I had decided that I would give my next gift to Tony. I wanted him to realize the dream that was lost so many years ago. I wanted his kindness to reach beyond the confines of the park and out into the vastness of the world. I would help Tony get off the streets. I would get him housing. I would help him enroll again in school. And I would be his friend, for life.

"Tony," I asked as the sun rose over Pittsburgh. "Can I give you a ride in Kindness One?"

"Yeah, that'll be cool," he agreed innocently.

"Where would you like to go?" I asked. "I want you to take me to somewhere that's symbolic for you."

He asked to be taken to his old school where he felt most comfortable growing up. "They believed in me there."

We drove through the early morning streets of Pittsburgh to the school building, where I told him my little secret.

"You know how I told you that I've been relying on the kindness of strangers to travel around the world? Well that was only half the truth. . . . Do you want to hear the rest?"

"Okay," he replied a little suspiciously.

"People who help me a tremendous amount and offer me kindness, well, I try and repay them."

Tony was still confused as I continued.

"I'll set up a home for you."

And then his mouth dropped.

"I'll set you up in a certificate program so you can learn to cook."

And tears filled his eyes.

"And I will be there whenever you need me."

For a moment neither of us said anything. I could hear a mother and her young son chatting away on their morning stroll, the rush of traffic in the distance, and finally Tony's voice cracking as he said, "Thank you . . . this is monumental . . . to go to school again . . . thank you."

And then as it really hit him, he began to laugh, "You are something else, Leon — you are crazy! You know, I'm 49 years old now, so I don't need a big house. I can survive like this if I have to."

I reached for his hand and looked deep into his eyes, "No Tony. You don't have to anymore." I wanted him to understand that his life was about to change. In a "whoa, did that just happen?" kind of way.

He nodded at me knowingly. I could feel his pain, the regret that came from years of accepting a life that was unacceptable. He had become comfortable with pain, reducing his own expectations and dreams to fit the hard realities of his life. Tony had so much to give, and he had never been given a chance. I wanted to see him fulfill his dream. And I wanted him to finally have a permanent place that he could call home. For all the material things I once thought were important, I saw in Tony what really was important: not clamoring for success or seeking what we don't have, but loving the things and the people we do.

Somehow in that moment, I was connected back to the man sitting at that cold desk in the London office. Maybe we weren't so different after all. Maybe we were really just two good people trying to find joy the best way we knew how. The only difference was that now I had much better teachers.

I hugged my new friend goodbye, the joy bouncing off him like sunlight.

As I guided Kindness One out of Pittsburgh and toward New York, I felt like a part of me was still back there with Tony. I had the clothes he had given me now in my bag. But more than that, I had been reminded again why I was doing this — to connect in ways with people that I otherwise never would. I had reached out to a stranger only to find him reaching right back out to me, and I knew that the connection I had made with Tony had just begun. I had just made a friend for life.

As I rode into New York City, I could feel the vibrations of Kindness One in every muscle and tendon and joint in my body. I had been riding for over a day, taking a rather long detour to see the famous city of Gettysburg before heading to the most famous city in the world: New York, New York. If I could make it there, I could make it anywhere, right? Though my thighs were shaking and my head throbbing, the cacophony of car horns and the hum of eight million people chattering around me encouraged me through to my final destination. I like dramatic entries, which is why I had naively decided that I must drive through Times Square, the epicenter of the city, and quite possibly the world.

Unfortunately, whatever adrenaline I had leaving Pittsburgh had deserted me by the time I crossed the border out of Pennsylvania. I had stopped to find a place to sleep, and by my sixth rejection, I began to question whether I should go on. Now, I know what you're thinking? *You just had that amazing experience, and it made you want to quit?* Well, to be honest, yes it did. Because though my experience in Pittsburgh had forced off my mask, it had also broken my heart.

Loving strangers is hard. Tony had reflected back to me all those deep fears of where I could end up, lost to an adventure I couldn't quite break free from, and disconnected entirely from the family I once held dear. The fear of being tether-less overwhelmed me. If ever there was a point where I could turn back and go home without too many questions or regrets, that time was now. I borrowed a kind stranger's phone to call Lina, telling her I was unsure if I could make it any farther than New York.

"It's already been such an experience," I tried to convince her. "Maybe all I really needed to do was cross America."

"Don't tell me you made us go through all that just to go to New York?" I could hear her holding back her annoyance, trying to disguise it as a joke.

"But maybe that's all I needed."

Once again, I felt like I was back in that infamous therapist's office, except this time it was Lina sitting beside me.

"I don't think so, Leon. I wish it was, but . . ." I could hear her breathe in before she replied, "I don't know, do you really want to give up before you've even started?"

I hung up the phone with that question echoing in my ears. *Do you really want to give up before you've even started?* And those were the words that pushed me through that beautiful sunny morning in New York. The trees of Central Park were in full bloom. Even the air smelled clean, despite the teeming traffic around me.

I doubt it will surprise anyone at this point, but finding a free room in New York City is harder than it looks. Looking back on it, Times Square might have made sense for dramatic purposes, but not necessarily for logistical ones. I kept meeting tourists staying in tiny, overpriced hotels, who might have felt for my journey but weren't necessarily willing to let me sleep next to them.

My closest chance came with a family from Torino, Italy. It was a mother and her two sons. They were visiting the Big Apple for a few days, but unfortunately, didn't have enough room in their hotel room for another family member. They did, however, give me their number and offer me a place to stay should I make it to Torino.

"Are you sure?" I asked. "Because I'll come to Torino then and take you up on your offer!"

"We will be happy to have you," the mother replied.

I began to walk down Park Avenue, far away from the mayhem of Times Square. And that's when I saw him. Now, I know most people probably wouldn't have zoned in on Taso as a likely prospect. He was a young lawyer in his mid-thirties, wearing a button-down shirt and a formal tie. But there was something about him that said, "I am more than the cubicle I work in."

After I explained my situation, Taso paused, clearly weighing his options before finally replying, "Well, the kindness-of-strangers part really speaks to me."

Taso thought about it for a moment, and said the one word I had been waiting to hear all day, "Sure."

I thought back to the park in Pittsburgh, to Gus, who had said, "Never give up, Leon. Sometimes in life, no matter what happens, we have to just keep going."

I waited for Taso to get off work, and then we went to his apartment in Midtown Manhattan. His wife was out of town on business, and after clearing it with her, he gave me a few minutes to relax before we headed out to what he called my "Farewell to America" dinner.

As we sat at a Greek restaurant, we started talking about New York. Taso grew up in Massachusetts but had moved to the city in 2001.

"Wow, that was a tough year to come to New York," I told him. "Were you here for 9/11?"

"I was," he hesitantly replied, his eyes growing darker. "I had just moved here a month before. It was my first year of law school. I was standing literally two blocks away and saw both planes hit."

He stopped, sucking in his breath, trying to find the words to continue.

"You saw both planes hit the towers?" I

78

asked, shuddering at the thought.

"I did," his voice grew quieter as he looked out onto the street. "I was standing so close that when plane two hit, when the fireball came out, it actually burned the hairs on our arms — that's how close we were."

I wasn't sure how to reply. Of course, I knew all the horrible details, had watched enough hours of CNN in the aftermath and every anniversary since to hear what people directly affected by the tragedy had experienced, but I had never actually met one of them. Watching the drama unfold on CNN is far removed from having your own skin singed by the blast of a terrorist's plane slamming into nearly a mile of steel. And yet like all humans, I could still feel that fear in my bones, that knowledge that in one instant, the world as we know it can be forever altered with little warning and no explanation.

"How did that affect you?" I asked. "How did it change you?"

Taso looked back at me, holding my gaze, "It changed everything because it was the first time you saw a city like this actually injured."

He thought about it before continuing, his eyes brightening at another memory, perhaps just as painful, but also filled with hope. "But what you also saw was a kindness that you never saw before. I walked all the way from the World Trade Center to Queens that day and was given water and food the whole way. The city really came together, and that was a pretty awesome thing."

I thought back to Tony, how in even the harshest conditions — maybe because they *are* the harshest conditions — we are forced to share. Maybe it's the luxuries of life that make us forget the necessities. I know I forget them time and time again. I get so caught up in the things I want that I forget to honor the things I have.

Taso smiled at me across the table, "I think people can still be that kind."

I think so too, Taso. I think so too.

CHAPTER THREE

"If music be the food of love, play on."
— William Shakespeare

The loud horn blasted above me on the ship as I stood along its railing, the sea spray already covering my face. It was time to say, "Adios, America!" because I was heading to Tarragona, Spain, only sixty miles south of beautiful Barcelona. The journey would take ten days. My heart was racing with excitement. If you haven't figured it out by now, I am in love with adventure. The thrill of the unknown, the boyish dream to sail the world and greet a thousand cultures, the freedom that comes with not knowing where you're going or how you're going to get there. And now I was about to cross the vast Atlantic Ocean on a container ship with no itinerary in front of me other than to one day (sooner rather than later, I hoped) make it back to Los Angeles.

As the ship headed out of port I saw the Statue of Liberty, reminding me of all the people who had come to America before me. As the son of two Greek immigrants, I had seen the fear and confusion of stepping foot on a foreign shore, having to learn a new culture, a new language, a new life. My transition from London to Los Angeles had really only involved driving on the other side of the road and exchanging my raincoat for a pair of sunglasses.

After following my dream to America, running from the home I had long fantasized of escaping, I was now doing that journey in reverse, returning to the world beyond — to the Europe where I was raised, to the Middle East where so many myths and legends and tales were born, to India and Asia and wherever else this journey might take me. I would be leaving my language, my culture, my identity, and I would be relying completely on the gentle kindness of strangers.

The boat passed downtown, where the new Freedom Tower loomed large. Like Miss Liberty, it also spoke a thousand stories with one shiny spire, a reminder of the two towers that had once stood there, and the rebirth that had finally begun. It was a new New York perhaps, one that was scarred in unimaginable ways, but also one that never, ever gave up.

I went inside my cabin as the ship moved away from New York and into the darkening night. And then I went to sleep. For the next three days, I passed the time sleeping and eating and reading. Though I desperately needed the sleep, if there is one thing I have learned in life, it's that an idle mind is the devil's playground. I decided I had spent enough days isolated in my cabin. It was time to get to know the crew.

I went to the captain and asked him how I could help.

"You will work," was his reply.

I spent the rest of my week helping in the engine room and on deck. Scrubbing. Painting. Toiling. But at least I felt like I was being of service. I had a purpose on that ship, and through that, I also began to make friends. The men on board were from all over the world — Israelis, Jamaicans, Ukrainians, and Russians, a smorgasbord of nationalities. They had left behind families and wives and mothers to work fifteen-hour days with no land or love in sight. And through that isolation, they created deep and powerful bonds, becoming not just colleagues, but confidants and friends. They became family, and they kindly invited me into theirs.

Every day, I would join Pasqual in the engine room of the ship. Pasqual was from Israel and had a wife and three beautiful girls, who waited patiently for him to come home to Tel Aviv. Many days, we worked in silence, forming a quiet respect for one another.

At the end of each day, I would go up to the bow of the ship and watch as the bright red sun sank behind the world's end. White puffs of clouds were scattered throughout the sky, and the endless blue water stretched across the horizon, slipping over its edge. I would breathe in the fresh ocean air, spotting other ships filled with other men passing in the distance, and I asked myself could I ever give this up? Many of the men I was with had children and wives back home, but I also knew that they were seamen; it was part of who they were. Was I any different?

As we chugged along to the second continent of my journey, the captain informed me that the crew wanted to have a barbecue in my honor.

I was humbled. Why in *my* honor? What had I done? The barbecue should have been in honor of the people at the shipping company who had opened up their corporate hearts and let me on the ship for free.

It should have been for the sailors who had taken time out of their day to teach me about their work. It should have been for the captain who was leading us all safely to shore. But I had seen *Mutiny on the Bounty* — there was no way I was arguing with a ship of hardened sailors.

We set up the tables on one of the upper decks of the ship, where we could see the wide expanse of sea around us. After eating, I stood up on my wobbly chair and gave a little speech: "I want to thank you all, especially the captain, for allowing me on board this ship."

The sun set behind me as the sailors relaxed into another beautiful night. "I know that I spent the first few days sleeping." I began, "But, when you put me to work, you made me feel like a real seaman. So I say, thank you to the crew!"

Everyone cheered me back. And I knew that this was what they were looking for on the ship — not just the escape from home, but the creation of a new one. The kind of home that didn't ask for commitment or demands, just hard work and rowdy laughter at the end of the night.

The next day, I woke up ready to place my two feet firmly on land. First, I just had to find out if the captain agreed. I headed up to the bridge. It felt like the closer we got to shore, the more anxious I was to get there.

"So are we close to getting to Europe?" I asked the captain, standing a bit too close to the imposing man, trying to get a look at his mapping system as though I would have been able to read the computerized blinking dots that kept us on course.

"Yes," the captain answered patiently.

"Are we going to see land?" I asked again, feeling my pulse quicken at the mere idea of the shore. After nearly ten days at sea, I didn't know if I could make it another hour. Suddenly, the last few days of endless horizons and hard work and sea legs were catching up with me.

"You can see land right now," he mentioned nonchalantly.

I looked out but could see nothing, and then I noticed that one of the first mates had a pair of binoculars. I nearly ripped them from his hands, feeling desperate for that long-missed view of terra firma. And there it was. . . .

"I can see land," I shouted, "Oh my God!! Land!"

I went wild. I had seen the tip of Africa. The endless horizon had come to an end.

Europe, here I come.

■ ■ ■ ■

Sometimes life is hard. There are days when everything goes wrong, people are mean, your mind attacks you, and you cannot — and I mean, *cannot* — find a clean public restroom anywhere in the city of Barcelona. I knew my trip would entail days like this, but somehow I thought my arrival in Europe, my own bloody continent, would be far more — how shall I put it? — *kind.*

Sadly, after hours of hearing the word "no" from locals and tourists alike, I sat down on a park bench and accepted the fact that Europe was not being very nice.

The only "maybe" I had received all day was from a pregnant woman who told me that she would have to go home and ask her husband if I could stay with them. After waiting for hours, day turning into night, I began debating whether I should just sleep on the park bench I was sitting on.

I hadn't eaten since late morning. The sun was gone. And now I was being stood up by a pregnant woman who clearly was not coming back.

I remembered when I first told Lina my plan, she asked me, "Well, what happens if you don't find anyone to help you?"

At the time I had scoffed — what a ridiculous and yet absolutely rational question.

I believed as anyone who is about to embark on a trip around the world with no money and no gas that things would inevitably work out. But as I sat there on that park bench, I began to wonder: What if they don't? What if no one offers me a place to stay, a meal to eat, a tank of gas? What happens if my trip ends on this park bench in Barcelona, and I have to go back to the shipping company and beg for them to pay for a flight back home? I looked over at Kindness One and couldn't imagine abandoning her to such a fate. After crossing the Atlantic Ocean, I had to find at least one person in all of Barcelona who would help me in my moment of crisis.

And then I saw him. Hercules was in his mid-twenties. And yes, his name was really Hercules. He looked like a student, but more than that, he looked like he was the kind of free spirit who wouldn't ignore my cause.

I opened with the only truth I could think of: "I'm stuck, man."

And that's how I found a place to stay for the night, and a meal, and a tank of gas, and more than all of that combined, that's how my faith was restored in the European Union.

I left Barcelona with the same joy I had felt driving out of Los Angeles. It was once again just Kindness One, the open road, and me. All it took was one person. All it ever really takes is one person to say, "I hear you, brother, and I'm willing to help."

Hercules was my one person, and he had given me the fuel to cross the rest of the world — or at least the better part of Northern Spain.

On the way into France I met an assortment of characters: a retired clown who put me up for the night, a single mother of six who thought I was a celebrity of some sort (blame Kindness One and the magic of yellow!). "C'est très magnifique," she kept repeating as I took some of her children on a spin in Kindness One before she offered me a tank of gas.

As I drove through the French countryside, I couldn't help but feel that I had just snuck across enemy lines. The English and the French aren't exactly BFF's (sorry about Waterloo, old chaps!). I hoped that where my British accent might fail me, Kindness One's yellow-y charm might help.

I drove into the small provincial French town, Aix-en-Provence, just north of the

French-Spanish border, and about two hours west of the notorious wealth of the French Riviera. And that's where things started to go, well, topsy-turvy again. I had been on Kindness One for over eight hours; my arms were numb; my legs sore; and let's not even talk about my "derrière." I hadn't found a meal all day and was beginning to worry that I was hallucinating — in general not a very safe way to ride a 1978 motorbike with serious mental issues. When I finally found a place to park my bike, I didn't even care that it was in an illegal spot.

I started walking through the local farmers' market to see if there were any crumbs of kindness to be had. There weren't. In fact, I was facing rejection left and right. Finally, I saw an Internet café. I was able to get the café to give me a few minutes on the Internet, but oddly enough, not even a croissant to eat. I sat down and decided to email Lina to let her know I had arrived in the old world. I thought maybe she would even be online, but I could see by her status that she wasn't.

My fingers hovered above the keys. I couldn't say anything. I didn't know what to say. Was it fair that every time I doubted this trip I called the one person who hadn't wanted me to go? I closed the laptop and left the café with time still on my card. I walked out into the square again, wondering if maybe I had overestimated the world's ability to care. Maybe I would have been better off just staying at home and not even bothering with this whole connecting-with-humanity business in the first place.

As I settled into my "woe is me" crescendo of self-pity, I couldn't help but hear far more upbeat music playing at a restaurant nearby. I moved to see two African men playing a wide array of instruments. They seemed to be filled with all the energy that I was now shamefully lacking.

The moment I saw them, however, all my worries deserted me. Their music floated above the café tables and across the courtyard where they played. But it wasn't just two men who knew how to play instruments. These men were playing with all their hearts. People were smiling in the square; a little girl was dancing to the music. The music didn't just entertain; it soared. As it weaved itself immediately into my psyche, I could hear a more intimate song, that of the adventurer's soul, of people who had seen too much pain and had traveled too far from home.

After they finished collecting money from the café patrons, I approached them. Both wore gently used clothes, but I could see that they prized the guitars that surrounded them.

"Guys, that was absolutely phenomenal," I said, unsure if they spoke English. "You literally just changed my whole day."

"Thank you," replied Finesse, the taller of the two. He had long dreads and a wide smile and the charisma of a man who loved to perform.

Knowing we at least shared a language, I continued, "If I had any money I'd give you some, but I don't. I just wanted you to know that was really beautiful."

I quickly found out that Finesse and Tchale, who was short and slight and less outspoken than his friend, were both from the African country of Benin.

I told them about my travels, and then basically invited myself to coffee with them. Thankfully, they agreed not only to chat with me, but to pick up the tab, too.

As we walked to a café together, Finesse told me, "Our dream is to one day become big stars — big singers, to get a message to people. A message of love."

Finesse and Tchale had been performing on the streets of the world for twenty years, surviving solely on euros tossed into hats and fees from the small gigs they were able to book, even sending money home along the way. But their real income was the love they derived from making music.

Some scientists say that human DNA can actually be reduced to musical notes, meaning that our whole being — the way we think, the way we feel, the way we act — is actually a previously written symphony, unique only to us. We have rhythm in our souls, but even more, we are literally made of music. Finesse and Tchale understood that, and they wanted to share that music with the strange and wondrous world around them.

We found a quaint sidewalk café with woven chairs and marble tabletops, and they offered to buy me lunch. Two practically penniless Africans taking me to lunch? Suddenly my crappy day was turning around. All those unpleasant thoughts I had about mankind were being reversed over a two-course meal of chicken and ice cream. After lunch, Tchale and Finesse invited me back to their small, one-bedroom apartment. They slept in the same bed out of necessity. It didn't take long for them to pull out their instruments, and engage me in a really terrible jam session. Not their fault at all, of course, but mine. Thankfully my terrible voice didn't prevent them from offering me a place to stay for the night.

The kind men gave me their bed, offering me an African nightdress in which to sleep. We all had tea as Finesse looked around their small living room, sitting on the couch they were adamant about sleeping on so that I could have a good night's rest.

As I found out, Finesse and Tchale had left their families when they were very young. They had been playing music in Benin since they were twelve, but there were no jobs for them there, and being a musician in Benin paid even less than being a street musician in Aix-en-Provence.

"Not as many tourists," Tchale joked.

They had rarely been back since, moving around Europe over the years. They never called any place home for longer than six months, until they had found this little apartment in the South of France, where they had found enough success to believe that they could do more than just survive: They could inspire.

"Sometimes, I think, should we go home?" Finesse explained, his voice weary. "But then I remember, we are carrying the music of our home to other people. How would we ever learn to speak the same language if we were not willing to leave our villages, our cities, and share our hearts with other people?"

"You are bringing them the music of Benin?" I asked.

Finesse leaned forward and said in the clearest English he could muster, "We are bringing them the music of love."

I woke up the next morning with my own spirit's rhythm humming within me. It didn't hurt that Finesse and Tchale were already outside on their patio, playing music. I joined them in the courtyard for breakfast when I heard a French voice calling down from above. There was no way that God could be French, and I'm not saying that just because I'm English. But it wasn't the voice of God, just Finesse and Tchale's neighbor Wilfred, who was intrigued by the men's bald visitor.

Wilfred explained, "They play music all day, every day. They work music; they live music. They don't play for themselves. They play for all the people."

He laughed a little before adding, "They play for the world."

The two men had long given up on returning home, but what they had received in return was the ability to connect with the world.

After Wilfred left, I shared with them, "To me, the fact that you are doing this, inspiring other people, is an inspiration to me. You know, when I saw you on the street yesterday, it was your music that made me come talk to you. Your music has touched my heart. And so have you."

The night before they had told me that the one thing they really needed in order to spread their message, in order to introduce themselves to the world, was a music video. Like with Willy, I realized I didn't just want to help people fill a need; I wanted to help them fulfill a dream. And their music was a dream worth hearing. Just like me, they wanted to make it around the world. They just needed the fuel to do it.

"And so," I continued. "I have decided to help pay for your video."

I could feel time slow as Finesse and Tchale realized what this gift could mean, what it might look like to see their hard-earned dream come alive. They looked at each other in total shock, and then they began chatting quickly in French. Although I had studied the *langue de l'amour* for nine years in school, I must admit I never learned a word. (Sorry Madame Beauvais and Monsieur Parfour.)

I could see that the two chaps from Benin were getting emotional. Tchale seemed the more stoic of the two, but Finesse had tears in his eyes.

Tchale looked at me and said two simple but powerful words, "Thank you."

"No, no," I replied, my own eyes filling with tears. "Thank you. It's passion like yours, not just for music, but for people, that touches everything. That changes others."

"You have changed us," Finesse replied.

"And you have changed me," I told him, knowing that should I ever question my journey from this point on, it would be Finesse and Tchale's music that would carry me along.

I remember months before I left London, I had a dinner with eight of my closest friends. I told them of my plan to travel to America, how I needed a change in my life. Only one person at that table believed I would do it. That person was me. The rest told me to stay put, that the feeling would pass. They didn't mean to shoot me down, but sometimes going out and changing your life is even more terrifying to those who can't.

I know that's why vagabond hearts scare so many people. It feels safer to have a family, to stay put, to let the need for adventure, or even connection, fade into the quiet comfort of a predictable life. And living for music, living your dreams, loving strangers can be scary.

Though I could have listened to my friends and stayed in that London apartment, miserable and static, I didn't give up on my dream. Che inspired me, and now, I was inspired by Tchale and Finesse. Inspired by their absolute commitment to doing what they loved, no matter the cost.

I walked from their house to Kindness One with that goodness pumping through my soul. As I turned the corner, I saw a small blue and white envelope on my bike. What could this be? A love letter in French? Not exactly. It was rather a very expensive souvenir from the chaps at parking enforcement. I told you those French didn't like the English. I had received my first parking ticket for 45 euros. Now what? I decided to keep the ticket as a memento, and if the French army wanted to chase me to India, they were more than welcome. I wasn't turning back — the music would play on.

CHAPTER FOUR

"The key is to keep company only with people who uplift you, whose presence calls forth your best."
— Epictetus

In many ways, the only reason you are reading these words is because of a life-changing meeting I had nearly twenty years ago. This probably comes as no big surprise, but my adolescence wasn't pretty. In fact, it was a rough couple of years before I became the only slightly less awkward man I am today. At home, I was the infamous middle child, stuck between two brothers who somehow had been given the manual on life that I failed to receive. The only respite I felt was when I was walking home from school. On that brief walk, I could be whoever I wanted to be — and that was often anyone but Leon Logothetis. But then I would get home, and whatever little self-worth I had would slip away between my much more boisterous brothers.

Thankfully, I have a good mother who noticed that things were not going so well for her middle son. She sent me to see Dr. Susan Mann, an after-school teacher of sorts. It was Dr. Mann who lifted me out of my slumber. She showed me two things: One, that kindness was everything. And two, that I was worth something.

"You are special, Leon," she would say as she sat across from me in her bright, window-lined office. "Your talent is unlimited."

Sometimes all it takes is one person to believe in you, in order to believe in yourself. The world is often much better at telling us when we are wrong or what we need to fix or how we've screwed up, but really all it takes is one person to look inside us, and tell us that we can be whatever we want to be, for us to believe. As I walked through the wealth-drenched town of Saint-Tropez, hungry and homeless, wondering again why I — once that gangly, pimple-faced kid — had thought I could pull off an adventure like this, I couldn't help but remember Dr. Mann's words, so many years after they were first uttered.

I had seen firsthand how believing in

someone else was not only the medicine I needed — it's the medicine the whole world needs. I saw it in Tchale and Finesse's eyes when I offered them the gift of the music video. I wasn't just giving them something, I was saying to them, *I believe in you. I have faith in your gifts. You are special, and your talent is unlimited.* We all need to hear those words.

Which brings us back to Saint-Tropez, the legendary French playground of the rich and famous like Bridget Bardot, Brad Pitt, and, more recently, the great man himself, Justin Bieber. As I drove along the French Riviera, I was sure that I was on my way to the best night of my life. I saw myself sleeping on a ten-million-dollar yacht, replete with hip-hop stars and some caviar. I envisioned David Attenborough narrating my experience in his thick British accent, "And here Leon docks for the night on the decadent yacht of Mariah Carey, enjoying fine Michelin dining and sleeping under two-thousand-thread-count sheets." I saw myself falling asleep to violins in the distance and awakening to the lapping waters of the French Mediterranean.

I did not fantasize that it would take me three hours just to get a free crepe for lunch. And sadly, nearly everyone else I approached either laughed at me or pretended they couldn't understand what I was saying. This was Saint-Tropez, half of them were from the UK or America, so I knew they spoke English. They weren't bloody fooling anybody with their "Non Anglais." I know you Anglais people!

They say those who have a lot give a little. I had been given much by those who had little, but despite what was happening that day in Saint-Tropez, I reminded myself that I had also been given much by those who had a lot. Because for every Tony, who lives on the streets, there is a Taso, who lives in a Midtown high-rise. Both of them had offered me hope.

I was wondering where to head off to next, and then I remembered I have friends in Italy. I opened up my magic bag and quickly dug out the number of the family I had met in New York City, the ones who were visiting from Torino. It had only been two weeks since I had been in New York, and yet it felt like scenes from a movie I had watched and not necessarily memories from my own life.

"Haha," I cried out to no one in particular as I pulled out the Italian family's phone number. Torino it was. I got back on Kindness One with a new verve. I revved that little engine and swung back out onto the highway. It would only take me seven hours. Surely I would find a bed there.

Seven hours later, Kindness One was running on fumes, and I was running on my last drops of adrenaline. We drove into the main square of the ancient town. Like most Italian piazzas, it had been a part of the city for hundreds of years, its stone structures worn smooth by time, a reminder of the millions of people who had lived there and long since gone. If you listened carefully, you could still hear the horse-drawn carriages clacking down the road.

Unfortunately for me, I was receiving little help in this Italian town. You see, in order to call my Torino friends, I needed to find a phone, and in order to find a phone, I needed to find someone who would be willing to let me use theirs. This was apparently a far more difficult request than I had anticipated.

Finally, I came across a local man who spoke English and seemed willing to hear me out. Ricardo was in his twenties with blonde hair and an easy demeanor, as though he were waiting to go out on that yacht I had been expecting in Saint-Tropez. He couldn't help me with a place for the night, but he offered to let me use his phone to call my Italian friends. Unfortunately, it went to voicemail, but then Ricardo offered to call a friend who lived about twenty minutes outside of Torino. He spoke to him briefly and explained my situation.

He hung up the phone, "Filipo says you come stay with him."

"What?" I asked, flabbergasted.

"Yes," he smiled, nodding with an easy smirk as though he did this all the time. My new Italian friend drew me a rough map and sent me on my way.

I was so excited I didn't even bother to ask him anything else. I had the man's name. Filipo. I had his address. Roberto Street. And I had a crumpled up piece of paper with a pathetic attempt at a map. Turns out, I was heading toward disaster.

I started riding, and then I realized the patently obvious: I was lost. And not just, "Oh, it's only around the corner" lost. I was Italy lost. Which meant I was in the middle of a field in the middle of the night in the middle of nowhere. I pulled over to look at the map again. Whatever road I was supposed to take I had clearly missed, and whatever road I was on, I couldn't find on the chicken scratches Ricardo had drawn for me. He said it was twenty minutes outside of town, but that was an hour ago. So I did what any good sailor does when lost at sea, I started to pray. Out loud. In a field. In Italy.

So um, universe, I'm really grateful for this map. And I am grateful to Ricardo for giving it to me, but I could really use your help right now. Because I'm lost. Like, really lost. And scared. In fact, as I'm sure you can see I am in the middle of absolutely nowhere. Don't get me wrong, I'm sure it's lovely during the daytime. I'm sure you did a great job, but I really have to get to this man's house because I want a bed. I need to sleep. I mean, I am the captain of kindness, you know? And the captain of kindness never gets lost!

I stopped and realized that whatever divine spirit might be out there may not respond to pride — it is one of the seven deadly sins, isn't it? I needed to change my approach. Maybe the spirits would respond better to pity?

Okay, universe, God, old chap. You see, driving this bike is not easy. It's very challenging. Emotionally and physically. It's very challenging. And to be lost in the middle of nowhere doesn't help, I am afraid. I don't know. Sometimes I honestly just want to give up and go home. All I really want to know is where Filipo lives. That's all. I'll do whatever you want. I'll become a Hare Krishna, and I will sell Kindness One at a scrap heap in

Delhi. Just help me find Filipo's.

I waited. And then I looked down at poor Kindness One, whose fate I had just bargained with.

Help me, Kindness One. You're my only hope.

Then in the distance I saw two bright lights. Either this car was going to save me, or it was going to run me over. At this point, I was willing to take my chances. I waved it down and asked a rather bemused Italian man for help.

"Hello, hello. Um, Roberto Street?" I gesticulated wildly, hoping that if my English confused him, maybe my arms would do the translating. Thankfully, my rudimentary knowledge of elementary school Latin allowed me to understand that he had no idea what I was saying, and even worse, that he had no clue where Roberto Street was. I decided to take a different tack.

"Filipo's! Filipo's!" I began to yell, waving my arms again in what I thought looked like "Italian Speak." And then the miracle happened.

"Filipo?" The older man asked, peering out of the car enough for me to now see his face. He had gray hair and the type of tired eyes that come from a long day at work.

"Yes, Filipo!" I cried, beginning to feel

those champagne bubbles of hope.

The man got out of his car and joined me in wild gesticulations, "Si! Si! Filipo's!"

To my absolute astonishment, this man whom I had met in the middle of a deserted street, in the middle of a deserted town, in the middle of a deserted field, actually knew the Italian stranger for whom I had been looking!

In broken English and a splattering of Italian, the man proceeded to explain where Filipo lived.

He pointed down the road to a small pathway that was covered by trees as well as by darkness. It had been right there all along, but I never would have found it.

"Grazie mille!" I exclaimed before returning to my native tongue, "Oh, thank you, thank you, thank you."

I got back on my bike and finished my prayer.

As I was saying, universe, you rule. Really you do. And so do you, Kindness One. And so does everyone on the face of this planet. We all rule. Wait, does that really mean I have to become a Hare Krishna?

As I approached the tall, metal gates of what looked like a rather large villa, all I could do was hope that my Italian friend had actually

107

sent me to the right place. Otherwise, I would be riding into a random man's house in the middle of the night. In America, I would most likely have been shot. In Italy, maybe strangled with spaghetti? All I knew was that it was too late to turn back. I opened up the gate and drove into the dirt yard that stretched across the front of the old house. I went up to the door and knocked. I looked around and waited. *Okay, universe, if Filipo answers, I will . . .*

But before I could make another bargain, the door swung open, and an older man in a crisp, button-down shirt and fine leather loafers came out to greet me. He smiled broadly as he announced, "Benvenuto, Leon!"

Filipo immediately pulled me into his house, as though we had known each other forever. I was just another good friend coming to stay the night, and I immediately felt at ease.

"Do you know how difficult it was to find you?" I laughed, still giddy from locating his darkened villa in the middle of a moonless night.

"Long road, huh?" he replied, his voice speaking of an empathy that I wished I were better at offering. It wasn't the "Poor Leon" sympathy I had craved as a child, but the,

"You will make it" faith that I hoped to give to everyone I met.

Filipo's cool only seemed to highlight my excitement as I offered him my tale, "I got completely lost for hours, and I didn't know where I was, and I stopped this guy in the car, and I said to him, 'Do you know Filipo?' I didn't think he would know you, but then he said, 'Yes' — well, 'Si!' — and he told me where you were, and I was like, 'This is just crazy.' And here we are!"

I was nearly out of breath, feeling the last few hours of stress coursing through me. Filipo chuckled and led me through his home, which had been in his family for three hundred years. Sculpted in stone with portraits of his ancestors lining the walls, the villa felt like an old museum, his ancestors looking down on us with stoic concern. Filipo had prepared a slap-up dinner, which in Italy means a feast.

We sat down in his wood-and-tiled kitchen and began to eat as he recounted the history of his family. With his gray hair and stately demeanor, he reminded me in many ways of my own father. When I was young, I always imagined that my father was a statue. He was so stoic, his posture so polished, that he seemed as though he had been cut from marble. But then, over the years, I watched as my father dropped his own mask. I think in many ways, because I did not fit in, he had to learn how to reach out. I wasn't polished marble, and in my own reflection, he realized, that surprisingly, neither was he.

As Filipo pushed a plate of burrata my way and refilled my glass with water, I could sense that he had perhaps experienced the same transformation. There was something about him that hinted at a changed man. He had been born in the legacy of wealth, but somewhere along the road, he had forged his own path. One that I could tell echoed my own.

He smiled gently at me and asked, "So how has your journey been thus far?"

I sighed, explaining to him, "I have traveled from Los Angeles all the way to here without spending a single penny."

"Fabulous," he clapped his hands together as though he had been watching the whole time.

I continued, "I've been relying entirely on people like you. On kindness."

I stopped, feeling that my simple explanation was disguising the far greater journey underneath. I set down my fork and continued, "Earlier today I was in Saint-Tropez, and here I am in a house built over three hundred years ago. Sometimes I feel that I am not in reality. Like I'm dreaming. Right now, I feel like I'm dreaming. It's like we're having this conversation, but I'm dreaming."

He smiled, "It's a lot of stress."

I sighed again, "The bike takes a lot of energy out of me. Not knowing where I'm going to stay takes a lot of energy out of me. Not knowing where I'm going to sleep."

He nodded with a knowing look, as though he too had traveled the world on a yellow motorbike with no money, adding, "It's a lot of uncertainty about what's coming along."

It was. It is. The world is an uncertain place, and often the only touchstone, the only marker we can find, is when another person actually stops us and says, "It's all going to be okay." I smiled, sharing, "It is, but when I get the opportunity to meet people like you and to sit in a home and to eat some food and know that I have a place to stay, the calmness returns. Even though I know tomorrow it's all going to start again. Right now, I feel held by it, by your kindness."

Filipo picked up a scoop of pasta and put it on my plate.

After the meal he suggested I go to my

room and get some much-needed rest. I lay down and thought again of Dr. Mann. She had given me the courage to not just be free, but to also be myself. To know who I am and to believe in that person. As Filipo and I talked that night, I realized that sometimes it only takes one person to convince you to go on — just one compassionate voice amongst the cacophony to once again set hope alight.

In the morning, I said my good-byes to my new Italian friend and continued heading east. This time I was off to Lake Como to search for George Clooney. I had promised Lina I would find Mr. Clooney and get his autograph (and his number) for her. On the way to Lake Como, I found some Italian Good Samaritans to give me gas, arriving soon after at one of the most beautiful places on earth. The sun was setting, and the lake was shimmering with the last rays of light. I had no doubt George would soon be on his way to greet me and my yellow bike, or at least someone half as nice.

But like that yacht in Saint-Tropez, George never appeared. Instead I spent the next four hours trying to find someone to open their home to me, begging hotels for a free room, cajoling people on the street to let me crash on their couch. I even walked into a church to try and find some love. Nothing. I was facing the real possibility of sleeping for the first time in the sidecar of Kindness One. From villa to "homeless," this was becoming a true riches-to-rags story.

There were throngs of people along the lake, enjoying the fine weather and the light breeze stirred up by the waters of Lake Como. I stopped a few more people, but it seemed that kindness was nowhere to be found. Maybe all the generous people were over at George's house. Sipping martinis and watching reruns of *ER*.

Unfortunately, it was going to be Kindness One for the night. I put on all the clothes I had and lay down in the sidecar. I tried my best to ignore the drunken Italians walking by, peering at the sleeping madman. I woke up with the rising sun. I crawled out of Kindness One and walked to the water's edge. Dangling my feet in the lake, I felt a burst of energy flush through me. I may not have had a home for the night, but I was fully alive. I was living my dream. I may not have connected with anyone in Como. But I was living my dream. I may not have had much gas in the tank. But I was living my dream — out on the open road, in the open lake, freed from all the masks and constructs I feared pinned me down at home.

I slipped off my trousers, remaining in my Union Jack boxer shorts as I dove into the water, taking one of my whenever-I-can-get-one baths in the majesty of the lake. The sun dawned just above the surrounding mountains, birds dipping down into the water, singing out to one another as they flew overhead. The once-busy town was now quiet as I swam in Lake Como.

I got out of the water, got dressed, and headed east again. I decided to stop off in the only town in Italy that didn't speak a word of English. This was not on purpose. I had no idea that the inhabitants of the entire little town of Portogruaro, nestled in the heart of Italy, have never learned even a word of English.

I decided to try the local police station. Surely they would help me. I was pleasantly surprised to find that the officer on duty spoke English (apparently, the only English speaker in town). I was less pleasantly surprised to find out that he did not like me.

"I am traveling around the world and need some help," I explained once I discovered we shared a language.

"Are you in danger?" the bored man at

114

the front desk asked. It didn't seem like he had much else to do, so I thought my tale of adventure might pique his interest. I explained my travels and that I was looking for some gas or food or a place to stay.

"Do we look like a hotel to you?" the police officer curtly responded.

"No, but —"

"No, but nothing, please leave," the officer concluded. Apparently, he was up to his ears in British travelers crossing the world on kindness and had no time for me.

I prayed that I wouldn't have to spend another night in Kindness One, careful not to bargain anything I wasn't willing to give. Surely the Italians would save me.

Finally, after pulling into one of many gas stops, I *was* saved. But not by the Italians. Bertha and Max were a Belgian couple crossing Europe in their RV. Not only did they offer to fill up my precious yellow bike, but they also let me sleep on the floor of their RV, which they had nicknamed "The Beast." Being rejected by the Italian police: embarrassing. The thought of spending another night in Kindness One: exhausting. Being saved in Italy by Belgians with a Beast: priceless!

In the morning, I waved good-bye to my Belgian friends after eating a breakfast of

115

pancakes and sausages. Pancakes and sausages? My luck was looking up. I drove through the green and winding countryside of Italy, heading east from Venice. The Italian Alps jutted up in the distance, their caps still covered in snow. A couple of hours later, I arrived in Trieste. Bejeweled in the colors of the Mediterranean, the blue sea sparkled below the tree-lined cliffs, while red-tiled roofs embroidered the sculpted town.

I drove into the heart of the city and threw the memory of my parking ticket shenanigans away as I parked the bike illegally, again. I knew that one day I would probably regret doing this, but I didn't have much choice. If the French army were already after me, what difference would it make if the Italians joined in?

The piazzas of Italy are all spectacular, but the one in Trieste seemed to stretch on for miles, bookended by the sea and the stately city hall. I thought surely someone out here might be feeling generous. A man slowly cycled past me on his bicycle, and I hoped that he might be one of them.

I stopped him with my usual bold but slightly delusional outburst, "I need someone to put me up in their house for one night."

Alex was in his early forties, with a head of prematurely gray but thick hair. He was dressed like a bike messenger, which I thought he might be. He stopped his bike, and looked me up and down before saying nonchalantly, "Okay."

Although that is exactly what I wanted to hear, I was a little taken aback. "Okay," I repeated hesitantly, asking him, "What does that mean?"

"That you can stay," he replied, smiling at my surprise.

"In your house?" I asked, still astonished by how easy this was.

Alex laughed, repeating himself more slowly, as though I were the one who didn't speak English, "I have a house. And you can stay in it."

Since Alex was already on his way home, I followed him through the narrow stucco streets of Trieste until we came to his apartment. There, he introduced me to his wife and young daughter. It didn't take long for Alex to share with me his other true love: fencing. Alex had once been a great fencing champion, spending his childhood and early youth competing in the ancient sport.

He no longer fenced professionally, and I could sense how, despite his obvious love and vivaciousness for life, he had lost a piece of himself because of it. He picked up his fencing sword and swiftly cut the air with it, leaving behind a faint trail of regret. We had coffee with his family, and then Alex persuaded me to join him in a fencing match on the streets of Trieste. It was a rather random sight, if I may say so myself. He dressed me up in full gear, and we left the apartment with our swords in tow. Though I had never fenced before in my life, Alex's passion for the sport was contagious. In many ways, he reminded me of Tchale and Finesse, his generosity stemming from the love that once grounded him, offering him not just a discipline, but also a deeper philosophy on how to live.

As we found a place in the center of town with a bustling contingent of foreigners and locals walking by, I started to train in the ancient art of repartee. I discovered that fencing isn't about striking your opponent; it's about understanding his motives. Because behind those large white masks, there is a dance taking place, and though you might not be able to see one another's faces, you can still feel each other's energy. And that is the art of fencing: feeling which direction your opponent is going to move before he takes that victorious step toward you. After an hour or so, we sat down at a coffee shop, where Alex bought me a much-needed lunch.

"When I was young," he explained to me. "I learned so much from the man who taught me, my fencing master. He teach me everything."

In Alex's broken English he described a relationship I knew well. In his fencing master he found someone who believed in him, who showed him that his talent was unlimited. I sat there as his eyes welled up with tears. It was evident that his fencing master had been the one to give him that connection to who he was behind the mask.

He described how the relationship had taken on a sacred form of family. "For me," Alex shared, "it was like a father because he teached me for fifteen years, hours of lessons every day. It was better than a father. I learned a lot from him."

Alex told me that ever since he left fencing, he had hoped to become a master himself someday. "To be a fencing master will be one of my dreams. Yes, I wish to be as Dario. I wish to transmit the same positive attitude for life and for the sport that I learn from him."

I smiled, already knowing my next gift. "So you want to give back to the kids what Dario gave to you?"

He paused before explaining, "Yes. But let me be honest — I learned from my winning, but I also learn from my defeat. It's easy to win. Sometimes it's not easy to be defeated. You put your problems under your mask, and in fencing whether you win, whether you lose, you still shake your hand with your opponent."

He looked down and as though it was happening right in front of me, I saw his own mask drop. The happy, gregarious man I had met in the square allowed me into the inner life that dwells within us all — the fire, the spirit, the secret places where we hold those dreams and those fears. I watched as he brought down the facade he wore behind the fencer's mask. I saw him not just as who he presented himself to be, but also as who he really was, and I wanted to honor both of those men.

That night, I had dinner with Alex and his family, and saw what a good teacher he was to his own child, spending time with her before tucking her into bed. I stayed on their couch, and then the next morning, Alex and I spoke over breakfast at his apartment. I asked him, "Do you still want to be a fencing master?"

Alex hesitated, "Leon, some people, they dream of things they do not have. And some, you know, they accepts the dream they do, the life they have now."

"But what if I said," I paused, trying to see how to offer this gift. "What if I could help you? I want to help you become a Master in Fencing. Whatever you need to become that. Whatever might help — classes, equipment . . ."

Alex stopped. He didn't say anything at first. Instead, he just looked down at the ground. If we had been in a fencing match, I would have had no clue as to his next move.

"Grazie, Leon," he nodded, "Really, this mean so much."

"I just thought if this is what you wanted to do and you —"

Alex cut me off, putting his hand on my arm as he explained, "No, please, it is very kind." He paused before continuing, "But it would not help me."

At first, I was confused, but then Alex explained, "You see, if I was to be a good master, that mean I would first need to take care for my student."

I nodded, trying to understand what Alex was saying. "You see, I know this young man, this student, and he is the one that needs help. Not me."

Alex explained that there was a young boy

who had lost his father and couldn't afford the clothes and equipment for fencing. Without someone stepping in he would be forced to give up the chance to become the man he was destined to be.

Alex finished arguing his case, "Because for me fencing master was kind of a father, sometimes better than a father, that I lost for a lot of years. I think that this could be a marvelous gift for Angelo, that he will now never see his father, but he will know forever a fencing master."

No one had yet asked that his gift be given to someone else. I was absolutely humbled by Alex's request, barely able to reply. All I could say was, "Done."

He gave me a long and heartfelt hug, "Thank you, Leon. Thank you very much, friend."

I walked back to Kindness One, happy to discover that she was ticket-free.

I got on my yellow magic friend, and we began to drive back through the city of Trieste, on our way out of Italy and into Bosnia. Life is filled with uncertainty, but one thing is certain: The universe has an interesting plan. Because if a shy, acne-riddled young boy hadn't met a kindhearted American Doctor in London all those years ago, then Angelo wouldn't have had the chance to continue his training. I was taught that by believing in others, we give them the gift of knowing how to believe in someone else. We break through the cacophony of criticism and fear, of heartache and insults, of the masks we are all forced to wear, and we remind each other that we are all special and that our talents are unlimited.

CHAPTER FIVE

"Smooth seas do not make
skillful sailors."
— African Proverb

I remember once reading a lecture that the great writer Joseph Campbell gave at the beginning of World War II. In it, he reminded his students, "Permanent things, of course, do not have to be fought for — they are permanent. Rather, it is our privilege to experience them. And it is our private loss if we neglect them."

My own grandfather fought in World War II, and I remember my father telling me stories about how at one point, many Brits truly believed that London would be destroyed, a city left in rubble, its people cowed under the tyranny of the Nazis. But though many brave men fought during those years to save the ones they loved, those permanent things — their histories, their cultures, their homes — could not be destroyed.

As I rode across Europe, heading out of Italy — the Alps to my north — and entering Slovenia, I couldn't help but think of all the wars that had marked this land. In many ways, there was far less history in America by comparison. Of course, war had happened — people had died on its soil — but the history of Europe was filled with centuries of turmoil. Too many people, too many nations fighting over their histories, their cultures, and their homes.

I made a pit stop in Ljubljana, the capital city of Slovenia. There, I stayed with a schoolteacher and his family. The only request was from his eight-year-old son, Janek, who asked that if I ever chronicled my journeys I would mention him. So, here you go, Janek. Thanks for letting me sleep on your parents' couch, and don't forget to be nice to your sisters!

From there, I continued on to Croatia, arriving in its capital, Zagreb. Again, I felt like I had left the modern world. Though new cars and trucks passed me along the road, the wooded forests and the hawks flying above were persistent reminders that, despite this country's history, the land beneath us had never changed. Driving into Zagreb, the old world was mashed right up against the new. Russian Orthodox church spires and leftover communist buildings mixed with the modernization of twenty-first-century Europe.

I pulled into the town center, parked Kindness One legally for once, and in record-breaking time, found someone to be nice to me — apparently kindness happens quicker in Croatia. I even met a finalist from Croatia's version of *American Idol.* Though she couldn't offer me a place to stay, she gladly sang me a song to ease the rejection. Afterward, she told me, "There is hostel just down the street. Maybe they help."

I figured anyone who can get on *Croatian Idol* must know what they're doing. I got back on Kindness One and located the hostel near the picturesque square that was the heart and soul of the city. Before I even made it to the front desk, though, I ran into a fellow traveler, Fraser, or, as I would soon be calling him, "The Scotsman." The Scotsman was a slight man with cropped dirty-blond hair and an easy smile. I told him of my journey.

He offered to buy me a coffee at the hostel's café, and as we sat and talked, I felt as though I were looking into a mirror. Fraser's love of adventure reflected my own desire for the road and all its magic and madness.

Fraser explained his plan to travel for the next four years by bicycle. "I just wanted to do something that I would look on for years to come and think, 'What an amazing experience.' And I'm just at the point in my life where if I don't do it now, I probably never will."

"It's funny, Fraser," I looked into my coffee as I spoke, as though I might see my future in there. "I have this wonderful woman back home, in LA, and I left, and some days on the journey, I don't know why I did, and then I have moments like this and I wonder whether I will ever be willing to give them up."

My new friend completely understood. As he explained, most of his friends and family were already married with children. "I'm not ready to settle down," he continued. "And I suppose I just realized that this is an opportunity I can't afford not to take."

This man was speaking my language. The purest form of Scottish known to man! He knew what it was like to attend weddings, be the best man, hold your brother's baby in your arms, and know that it just wasn't your time yet. Know that it might never be your time, that finding a soul mate in a hostel in Zagreb, meeting musicians from Benin on the streets of Aix-en-Provence, driving through Nebraska and Slovenia, and crossing the Atlantic Ocean might be the most permanent things in the world. Life on the road provided its own home. But as I drank the rest of my coffee, I couldn't help but wonder, at what price?

Fraser explained, "I think that part of the problem is if you're not passionate about something, there's only so much you can give. I'm passionate about this, so . . ."

His voice cracked, the emotion seeping through. I understood. It was the joy that comes when you finally stop living the life others have given you and you start living the one you always dreamed might be yours. The French philosopher Voltaire once said: "Man is free at the moment he wishes to be."

Fraser would be gone for four years, a far greater length of time than my own adventure, but he wasn't running away. I knew that. He was committing instead to that great and open road of self-discovery. Sadly, so many of us live behind the mask of "Everything's fine," and we never get to ask the question, "What if?" What if I followed my dream? What if I learned to play the violin? What if I started rowing on the weekends? What if I traveled the world on a motorbike with only kindness to carry me? I knew Fraser would find that the road was not an easy one, but the one thing it did promise was the ability for us to accept our own fates. It showed us that we would never have to ask, "What if?"

I drove out of Zagreb and headed toward Sarajevo, the capital of Bosnia-Herzegovina. It was only a five-hour drive, but Kindness One was beginning to act up for the first time since that breakdown in Chicago — less than five thousand miles and yet so many memories ago. The bike would trick me into a false sense of security, moving along nicely, only to conk out in the middle of a cliffside road. Not terrifying at all, I tell you. The five-hour drive turned into a ten-hour one, and I still had seventy-five miles to go as the sun set across the Bosnian countryside. It took me a number of gas stations before I found someone willing to offer me shelter for the night, a young couple who kindly loaned me their couch and some much-needed rest.

The next morning, I finally arrived in Sarajevo, which was described by one of the locals as the "Jerusalem of the Balkans." I soon understood why. Mosques, churches, and synagogues all live side by side, just as they have for centuries.

It was in Sarajevo that I met a Bosnian named Edis. Though I had decided that most of my journey would be free of tourist attractions, choosing instead to get to know a city through its people rather than its museums and castles, Sarajevo's rich history had always fascinated me. As in many of the cities I had already wandered, walking through Sarajevo's cobbled streets connected me to a past that seemed to rise up from the boulevards, calling out from the stone walls and towering trees of eras gone by. History had come to life. Though Sarajevo will always be linked to the dreadful wars of the 1990s — especially the siege that strangled the city from 1992 to 1995 — it is also the city where the Archduke Franz Ferdinand was assassinated along with his wife in 1914, lighting the fuse of World War I. The city's history runs through it like lightning, leaving the air taut as the most recent memories still try to settle.

As I drove through the streets of Sarajevo, I realized that it was the first city I had been to that had seen a war during my lifetime. As I passed the infamous Holiday Inn hotel, which sits directly on the street known as "sniper alley," I could still feel the fear that so many must have felt while crouching down in the guest rooms as shells slammed into the yellow facade of the hotel. I could sense the terror that the locals must have experienced walking down the main road, hearing the sound of sniper's bullets whistling past their ears, or even worse, striking. And here I was, only twenty years later, driving down that same street on a yellow motorbike of kindness. And despite the permanence of things, time does indeed change us — sometimes for the worse, and yes, sometimes, if we allow it, for the better.

I had heard of a local museum that told more of the story of the Bosnian War, but this was no ordinary museum. It actually used to be a house, the site of an underground tunnel that served a critical role during the siege of Sarajevo.

And in that house was its former inhabitant Edis, a Bosnian not far from my own age, who explained how the eight-hundred-meter tunnel had been built to give the city's inhabitants a lifeline during the siege, a lifeline during a time when humanity had turned against itself.

"So who owns the house now?" I asked Edis, who had grown up in the war, even serving as a soldier for a time.

"The government, actually. Although this was my family's house before the war," he explained. "We were here at that time, you know, when they came to build the tunnel. My father agreed to give the house and land and everything we had at that time for the army, for the tunnel."

It's not every day you meet a hero. Edis's family had risked their lives for their fellow neighbors, handing over everything they had to the army so that others might be able to get out of the city safely, and all the while, they had to pretend that they were living a normal life, in a normal house. They had to hold up the ultimate mask that everything was fine, even though they were playing a pivotal role in the middle of a major war. They had offered people a way out, but more than that, they showed them that the bonds of love and trust could not be destroyed by warfare. They were more permanent than anything else.

"So how does it feel to know that your house and your family helped to save the city of Sarajevo?" I asked.

"An incredible feeling," Edis replied. I could feel his pride. As much as I always looked at home as something that held me back, I could see that for Edis, it was what held him together. I loved the road less traveled, and yet so much of this world demanded permanence, demanded commitment, demanded valor in order to keep safe the places we call home and the people we call family.

We were standing in the tunnel itself, and as he looked into the darkness, where people had run quietly (and quickly) through the night, praying to make it out alive, Edis explained, "You know, I was also at that time defending the city. I was a member of the Bosnian army. I participated in this tunnel also. Here, we help three hundred thousand people to survive."

I could feel him looking at me in the dark, his eyes shining brightly as he said, "This is really a special thing."

For all my love of living life on the road, this man's family had taken an immense risk to stay, to commit themselves to each other and to their people. I thought again of my grandfather, who had risked his life to defend his own home.

My throat tightened as I realized out loud: "You are in very many ways responsible for saving this city."

Edis didn't reply. He just nodded.

Often it is so hard to accept gratitude, to honor ourselves for the good we do. But we must — we must celebrate what's permanent. Because though sometimes we can be a destructive people, sometimes we can be heroes.

Edis went back upstairs as I went for a walk in what remained of the passageway. I touched its cool, damp walls and felt my feet walking in the same footsteps of the hundreds of thousands who fled through it, praying that they might live to see the sun rise, that they might get to hold their wives once again or kiss the faces of their children, people for whom home wasn't a choice, but a desperate and heartbroken dream.

As I left Edis's former home, I thought again about my grandfather in London, but also back to Taso's story of 9/11 in New York. Wherever there is tragedy, there is also love. There are people coming together to save each other, to offer food and water, and in the case of Edis's family, to put their own lives at risk to protect what matters most.

Though I knew that there was still much healing to be done in Sarajevo, as I left Edis and walked back to Kindness One through the safe and quiet streets, I saw a people reunited — Muslims and Christians sharing the city in peace. And underneath that history of war, of destruction, of the assassination of Franz Ferdinand, was also a place of healing.

■ ■ ■ ■

I left Sarajevo for the hilly and beautiful terrain of Montenegro, taking a small mountain road that had been suggested to me by a young couple in the capital. Controlled by the Slavs, the Romans, and ultimately, the Soviets, the land that is Montenegro has struggled for centuries to find itself. The more countries I visited, the more I began to view them as people. Some, like France, were confident in their identities. Others were still reeling from recent traumas, trying to figure out who they might be in times of peace.

I rode through one of the many mountain passes that twist and turn through Montenegro only to realize I wasn't going to make it much farther without gas. The bike started sputtering, and I switched it to reserve, barely making it to a mountain village. After meeting a number of townsfolk who didn't speak English, I finally came across one who did. Sal had lived in New York many years before, until he ran into some problems with the chaps at immigration, who had *politely* urged him to return to his homeland.

"You go to restaurant in town," he offered,

showing me on my map where I might find this local establishment, "and talk to my nephew. Bekim. He maybe help you."

I arrived at the small café, where, once again, no one spoke English. But I was able to figure out one thing: Bekim was not there.

I sat down outside and began preparing to spend the night in Kindness One. I could feel a chill entering the air and already knew my night would not be as pleasant as the one in Lake Como. Not that my night in Lake Como had been particularly pleasant.

And then a small and sturdy man walked up to me. He spoke in thickly accented English: "I heard you're looking for me."

"Are you Bekim?" I asked.

"Yeah. Sal tell me you're traveling with your bike. You had some problems or what?"

Major problems, I thought to myself, and then I remembered all the stories I had heard so far along my journey — my sea mates being separated for months and years from their loved ones, the young fencer whose father had just died, the story of Edis and his family's sacrifice for their people. Maybe my problems weren't so major after all.

"I've basically run out of gas, and I'm on reserve. You're like an angel. I'm serious. I've been sitting here so long . . ."

Bekim smiled sheepishly. Shrugging his shoulders, he offered me gas and a place to stay. I had no hesitation in hugging this random Montenegrin man. Joy sometimes does that to me. I wasn't all that surprised to learn that Montenegrin farmers aren't big on hugs. Vodka, yes. Hugs, no.

We drove to Bekim's farm, where I met his whole family. Bekim showed me around his land as he explained, "I am a farmer. My father was farmer. For thousand years, we farm this land."

At first, I didn't believe him, or thought the number was lost in translation. "A *thousand* years? Are you sure?"

Bekim looked at me as though I had just questioned the color of the sky. "Yes," he explained. "A thousand years, twenty generations, my family work this land. It is ours. And we, how you say, we belong to it."

Well, talk about permanence. Wars had been fought, conquerors had come and gone, the world had changed, and here Bekim's people remained on the same land through it all.

As Bekim explained to me, his family only had one main source of income: their lone dairy cow. A thousand years of farming this land, and it was barely giving them enough to survive.

Bekim and I sat in his yard, looking out at his field as he explained what the land meant to them, even if he had to work in a local restaurant to make ends meet. "We are connected with this land like blood and meat together, you know?" Bekim explained. "You understand, like we are born over here; we are grown over here; and we die over here. We can't live without it."

"I can feel that," I told him. "You know, in the Western world we all live with our iPhones, with computers, with Facebook, with Twitter."

"No, it all over here also."

"Really?" I asked, almost forgetting that Bekim was my peer. In fact, he was even younger than I, and yet in many ways, he felt like he had been a part of this land since its beginning.

"Yeah, but not like the other places," he assured me. "We don't have time for it every day. We have to work our land, and at night when we go home we are tired, very tired, and we have to rest and sleep. We don't have time for computers."

Together, we looked back out at the land — how much history had passed over it, from kings and queens to Soviet troops and Bosnian rebels, to MTV and the iPhone. Years ago in London, I came across a preserved building from World War II near Farringdon Station. Its walls were in ruins, the roof long gone, yet life teemed around it. People were heading to work. Children were walking with their parents. History changes, but the routines of our lives remain the same.

Eventually we headed back into the house, and as the sun went down, I fell quickly to sleep, overwhelmed by the ghosts of history and another hard day on the farm.

After breakfast the next morning, I convened a small family meeting. Bekim sat in the middle of his couch with his wife next to him. His father sat on another chair, and his mother sat close by. And I stood awkwardly in front of them like an actor about to give the worst performance of his life.

As I explained my trip, Bekim translated for his family. They all nodded as I thanked them for their kindness, and then I took what seemed a dangerously long and deep breath before adding . . .

"I would like to buy you a cow."

Bekim didn't say anything at first. And then he finally translated it to the rest of the family. Suddenly, the whole group began to cry out, "Kráva! Kráva!"

I couldn't tell if they were happy or if "kráva" was an ancient war chant, but then

Bekim got up. With tears in his eyes, he walked toward me and hugged me. And he didn't let go. His family was still crying out, "kráva," behind him, and this time, I was the one being nearly bowled over by another's gratitude.

Finally, he explained, "Buying us a cow, that will help our family more than you can imagine. You see, having one cow is like a store for one family. You have milk. You have cheese all the year. But with two cows, you have store for other people. You go to the market; you sell your cheese, your own milk. You have bought us a store."

I smiled at his family and began to repeat the word, "Kráva?"

Bekim laughed, "Yes, Kráva. This means cow."

And so together, we all began to chant, "Kráva. Kráva."

I was going to buy them a cow.

I drove off that morning and saw Bekim's family standing in my only good rearview mirror, the other still tucked into my backpack, after losing it on the mean streets of Delta, Colorado.

I had started in Hollywood. I was now in Montenegro. I had begun to see the history of the world in motion, the past and the present forever trying to renegotiate the future. And the thread that moved through it all spoke to what mattered most. Home isn't just a collection of memories and fears; it is also the most permanent thing we have. It is the harbor in our storm, and sometimes the only thing worth fighting for.

CHAPTER SIX

"When the world says, 'Give up,' Hope whispers, 'Try it one more time.' "
— Author Unknown

"You must please feed the children of my family."

Unfortunately, the border guard's eyes weren't as sympathetic as his plea. They were bloodshot, and by the way he was swaying and holding onto the immigration counter that separated us, I could tell he was drunk. *Very* drunk. I could also tell that he was hoping that this weary English traveler on a yellow motorbike might be willing to pay a small bribe for entry into his country. What he didn't know was that this English traveler was extremely poor at the moment.

"I am traveling around the world, with no money," I said sheepishly. "So I have no money . . ."

This pissed him off. He tried his best to pull himself up from his drunken stupor, spitting the words out as though they tasted bitter, "Bike no come to Albania."

Bike no come to Albania? These were not words I was prepared for. How was I going to make a drunken border guard understand that if he didn't let me through my entire journey would be over? *Over!*

The only thing I could think of was football — or as the Americans call it, soccer — the most popular sport in Europe, including Albania. I started to talk to my soon-to-be BFF all about "the beautiful game," asking who his favorite team might be.

"Manchester United!" he shouted, as though celebrating a goal right in the heart of a football stadium.

"Yes!" I cried. "Manchester forever!"

And in those words, our budding friendship began. No one had to know that I was actually a Liverpool fan. Thankfully, I knew enough about my archenemies, Manchester United, to convince Mikos of our mutual love for all things Manchester.

"My friend, we like you," Mikos shouted, his preferred form of communication, it seemed. "Welcoming you to the Albanian home!"

I thanked him and quickly left the border crossing before he changed his mind.

I had never before been to Albania, but I realized one thing very quickly — Albanians are very proud of their heritage. They are deeply connected to who they are as a people, and there's a fierce pride that comes from that connection.

As I drove to the closest town, I found myself wondering about my own "home." Would it always be England, the place of my birth? Would it be Greece, the home of my ancestors? Or was it now Los Angeles, where so many miles away, my house and girlfriend and dog all waited for me to return — hopefully in eager anticipation. Maybe because I felt so disconnected from home, I decided to jump on the Albanian bandwagon and get a tattoo of their national flag. Well, sort of.

I was walking down the main street of the small border town when I saw the distant light of a ramshackle Albanian tattoo parlor. After discovering that the two tattoo artists inside spoke English, I asked them what kind of tattoo I should get. Their suggestion: the Albanian flag, *on my neck*.

"Guys, my girlfriend might not like that too much," I explained.

"Why not?" the younger brother who

worked at the parlor asked, as though there might be something wrong with my girl-friend.

"Well, unless she's secretly Albanian, she'd probably be confused."

I waited, expecting some sign of under-standing before I finally threw my hands in the air, and sighed, "Women!"

This they understood, and offered an alternative plan: a henna tattoo of the Albanian flag on my leg.

A henna tattoo on my leg, I could do. Lina might have more to say about an Albanian flag on my neck.

In the morning I headed off to Pristina, the capital of Kosovo. At first glance it's a bleak-looking place, with concrete remind-ers of the uniformity of the Soviet era scat-tered throughout the city. The heavens opened up, and rain was pouring down from heavy gray skies that matched the buildings below it. Cars and scooters and bicyclists crowded the rain-soaked streets, honking and yelling against the onslaught of traffic. I worked my way through, praying that Kind-ness One would behave while I sought a safe place to find some food and shelter and rest. And that's when I ran into him. President Bill Clinton.

Or more like the henna tattoo version of

him, because there in front of me stood a large imposing statue of the forty-second president. In gold. Probably not solid gold, but you never know. I made an illegal U-turn to ask a local about the statue. I met more than a local, though — I met a new friend.

Eleonora could have been any Western woman in any Western city. She was in her forties, wearing blue jeans and a fashionable blazer. The only thing that set her apart was the colorful hijab she wore on her head. She crossed her arms and looked up at the statue with me. She explained why Bill Clinton was standing there, "Usually our statues are for dead heroes, but Mr. Clinton helped our people a lot."

As we began to walk down the street, she explained to me, "Thanks to him and the others, we are in freedom now. We are independent now for five years."

Like Edis, Eleonora couldn't have been far from my age, and yet she had experienced so much — the horrors of war and the pride in the independence that followed. We walked through the heart of Pristina, the rain subsiding. As we walked she pointed out the different parts of her city to me, offering up the history of her country and her people — ethnic Slavs who had converted to Islam under Ottoman rule. As she spoke, I was reminded, again, of why I was making this journey. It was for these moments — these random encounters on rainy afternoons. I was not only meeting someone new, but also getting to know an entire people, and their history.

Eleonora took me to a local mosque, where we sat down inside. Like Edis in Sarajevo, she also had her own story of war.

Her voice grew quiet as she told me: "My family, they were taken by the Serbian forces . . . police actually . . . and they sent them to Lartse. It is the border between Macedonia and Kosovo. My family, they were sent away on trains."

Her eyes began to glaze over, as though she were watching the terrible scene unfold in front of us.

Finally, I asked, "Where were they sent to?"

Her face grew dark, her pain heavy and palpable, like humidity. She spoke in a strained whisper as though it was too hard to say, "To the camps."

She looked at me, life burning in her eyes once again, "It is something that nobody wants to happen again. Not here, nowhere else."

I was ashamed for all of us. That at the

sunset of the twentieth century, there could still be concentration camps in Europe. Never forget, they said after World War II, and yet less than fifty years later, we had to learn the same lesson again.

Stories like Eleonora's made me wonder if it's just *too hard* to love people. If having a family is really just making yourself vulnerable to the inevitable pains of life lurking around each and every corner. Maybe I wasn't running. Maybe I just didn't want to be hurt.

She cleared her throat, trying to sweep away the pain that filled the quiet mosque, "But not all of the people did bad things to everybody. Most of them were police and the private military, but not the people." She touched her heart as she continued, "The people did not commit those crimes. So we learn to forgive. We must remember that no matter who we are, where we come from, we are human first."

We sat in silence for a while. I looked around the beautiful mosque, which still had pieces missing from being bombed in the war. As much as Eleonora spoke to the hope of peace, I couldn't help but wonder: How do you forgive when your families are stolen in the night? How do you forget when what you hold sacred is shattered to pieces, and the life you once knew simply gone?

I know that all of us have good and evil in us. We are all capable of hurting others — some on grand scales, many more on small ones. And it all comes back to the same flawed idea: that somehow one person is more important than another. I know that for a long time I was mired in that selfishness. I only thought about myself, about what I wanted. I lived in the lonely belief that my feelings were somehow more important than those around me. And then one day I woke up in so much pain; I realized that the rewards of my selfishness would never outweigh the pain of isolation.

As we left the mosque, serendipity brought me up close and personal to someone who had truly lived and embodied selflessness. Mother Teresa. Or should I say a statue of the great lady. Bronze — not gold.

I'd admired Mother Teresa as much as the next chap, but I had never really learned too much about her. And then suddenly, I found myself in front of that statue, and I was absolutely mesmerized. Maybe that's the point of building these permanent fixtures — to forever inspire others by reminding them of the paths that some have chosen. I had always assumed Mother Teresa was an Indian woman, but as I found out that day, she had gone far from home in order to carry out her work. Because Mother Teresa was actually of Albanian descent — I knew there was a reason I got that tattoo!

Born in Macedonia, she left her people for Calcutta at the age of seventeen because she wanted to be of service to those who suffered most. She believed that it was only through loving one another that we might ever find love within ourselves. She had given up her home for a different vision of reality, for her dream to help the world. I looked up at the statue, and I knew right then, as I knew my own name, that I would do everything in my power to go to Calcutta. I wanted to see what this woman had accomplished by making the whole world her family.

I left Kosovo and rode into the country of my parents' birth: Greece. I used to spend my summers in Greece and was looking forward to spending some summer nights in the Greek heartland. After crossing the border I was thankful not to have to feign love for Manchester United with any drunken border guards. Instead, I sailed through and right into the northern town of Thessaloniki.

And then the wind went out of my sails, or rather, the wind went out of Kindness One. I was planning to head east to Turkey and cross the Bosporus Strait to Asia, but my little yellow friend had other plans. I was driving through Thessaloniki, looking out at the sea, feeling the quiet air around me. The pains of the war ravaged countries I had only just visited felt so distant here, lost against the lapping clear blue water.

After being treated to some food and gas, I hopped back onto Kindness One, only to have the bike stop in the middle of the street, in the middle of traffic, in the middle of a herd of honking, angry Greeks. Did I ever tell you that I don't really know how to fix a bike? I think I did. But I will tell you again. For dramatic purposes really.

I don't really know how to fix a bike.

I pushed my bike off the main road and began asking people where the nearest mechanic was. No one seemed to know. Finally, a local shopkeeper suggested that I go down a little alley, where I would find a mechanic. A good one in fact. Before I left, the shopkeeper added, "He likes money."

He likes money? Well, let's see how much he likes someone without any.

I met Gianni. And Gianni met me. I told Gianni about my problem. Gianni didn't

151

seem to like where my story was going.

He looked at me and then he looked at Kindness One, disapproving of both. "Why you go with yellow bike?"

I smiled. Trying to be as upbeat as possible as I explained, "Because it makes people happy."

He grunted at my response, so I thought I would hit him with my proverbial left hook: "And when people are happy, they do nice things."

He walked around the bike, tinkered with it for a minute, and then stood back and replied as though he were ordering a coffee, "One thousand euros."

One thousand euros! I tried moving the conversation to my rudimentary Greek, but that didn't help much either. Apparently, it would cost a thousand euros in any language. I explained my journey again, but Gianni just shrugged his shoulders and went inside. Well, so much for Greek solidarity.

I continued to wheel my bike through the streets of Thessaloniki and realized that, in my shock at Gianni's quote, I had forgotten to ask what was wrong with the bike!

More people started honking at me, and a few even started yelling again — my people really love to yell. All I needed was to find that one person willing to help me out. In the end, I found three. The first was an old Greek chap who helped push the bike out of the road and onto the path of another mechanic, who became my second angel. Once I arrived there, I met my third: an American woman who was getting her car fixed.

Spiro was a gentler mechanic than Gianni, listening to my explanation with compassionate eyes. After I was finished, he smiled: "Let's me look."

He knelt down and tinkered just as Gianni did, and finally stood back up. "Your plug sparking are badness," he explained.

"Can you fix them?" I asked.

He shrugged his shoulders, "I fixing cannot do fully for you."

I asked him if he could fix it at all, and he said that he could do a patch-up job. A patch-up job was fine by me, as long as it was a free patch-up job.

I walked out to where Anna, the American woman, was waiting for her car.

"Have you worked with this mechanic before?" I asked her, explaining my dilemma. "Do you think he might do it for free?"

"He might," she replied. "But let me ask him."

Anna came back out of the shop with a

big smile on her face. "He said to give him an hour!"

Give him an hour! I would have given him a week!

As I waited for the bike, and Anna for her car, we began to talk about my journey. Anna's parents were also from Greece, but she had been raised in America. Though she had lived her whole life in Chicago, she felt that it was her parents' homeland that felt most like home.

"What about you?" she asked.

"What about me?"

"Where do you feel at home?"

I laughed as I looked around the mechanic's shop, a snapshot of Greek life. Finally, I replied, "I'm still trying to figure that out."

Once our respective vehicles were ready, Anna asked if I needed a place to stay for the night. As she explained, "I don't really do this, you know. Let strangers stay with me, but I think what you're doing is really brave."

Most days I didn't feel brave. But I was happy to pretend if that meant I had a place to sleep. I followed her up to her house in the hills high above Thessaloniki. As we had dinner overlooking the sparkling city below, I told her about my journey: "I have a lot of experiences. I meet a lot of people, like you for instance, but it's very, very draining. *Very* draining."

And then I found myself saying more than I had to most people I had met along the way. I found myself telling her about Lina, "I know she'll still be there. Well, I guess I hope she'll still be there. Lina said I was just running, but . . ."

She smiled warmly from across the table, "Well, are you?"

I finally said the words that I had wanted to say to Lina, "I don't think that following my dreams has to be the same thing as running from reality."

Anna leaned back and asked, "Have you ever read *The Odyssey*?"

It had been a while, but I remembered Homer's tale of Odysseus who spent twenty years at sea, fighting to find his way home. How his wife, Penelope, rejected suitor after suitor waiting for him to return. And I remembered that there were many times on Odysseus's journey when he wasn't sure if home was where he really wanted to be.

"Maybe you just need to complete your adventure," Anna said. "To really appreciate what you have at home."

Anna continued, "I think we change by meeting other people. I can only imagine how much you've probably changed."

I wasn't sure what to say. As I thought about it, I realized that every time the trip had gotten too daunting, it was Lina I had called. It was our home in Los Angeles that I imagined returning to. Was I really just repeating a story that had been told so many millennia before?

And yet here I was on the other side of the world, once again finding that wonderful connection that marked the map of my journey just as surely as any city. But what happens after Odysseus goes home? Homer failed to write about that part!

I took a bit of the food Anna had kindly laid out for us, and told her, "I guess I'm still learning what exactly this whole trip means. I started out thinking I knew everything. Now, it's like the more I learn, the less I actually know."

She laughed, "I wish I could go with you on the bike."

"But you can," I told her, remembering the first day of my journey, when I realized just how possible the impossible could be. "See, that's the idea. Everyone can do this to some extent. It's about how we connect, not just where we connect."

I had begun to realize that leaving home might be the only way the world would ever make sense to me. It was by seeing how we were all alike that we would finally realize that no one person was more important than the other. And then maybe I would return with a different heart. One that understood better how to love.

Apart from the traffic, Istanbul is a magnificent city. I had made it through the Turkish border with my visa in place and no unnecessary hassles with the bike, arriving in the colorful city by early afternoon. I found my way to a local Turkish bazaar and tried to haggle a place to stay for the night. I was not having much luck. Most of the vendors wanted to sell me something, not help me, and as one tourist explained, "My husband wouldn't be too happy if I brought a strange man back to our hotel room." Well, I could understand that.

Things were not looking good.

But then I bumped into Mehmet. Mehmet wore aviator sunglasses and a black T-shirt, and seemed like the kind of guy who was always rushing off to an important meeting. After he heard my story, he nodded his head and quickly pulled out his cell phone. In Turkish, he had a brief conversation and then hung up. He told me to go to his cousin's house, where I could stay for the night.

"His name is Nasuh," he explained. "And I think you both will become quick friends."

All along this trip, I had asked people to trust me. Trust me for a tank of gas or a place to eat. Trust me to stay in their house. Trust me to stay with their wives and children. But I had also learned to trust. Like with Tony in Pittsburgh or finding Filipo's villa in Italy, I had discovered that the simple act of trust could turn into the foundation of friendship.

I arrived at Nasuh's house and was greeted at the door by an older Turkish man. Nasuh was a slim, stately gentleman wearing a sports coat and beige trousers. Like his cousin, he was clearly a businessman. But as I quickly found out, he was much more than that. Nasuh was responsible for saving thousands of people from natural disasters. Whenever there was such a tragedy, he would go with his team and save people trapped under rubble or mud.

He explained to me, "We don't do it for profit. It's only there for saving as many lives as possible during disasters and accidents, especially in the wilderness. Also, we educate people for disasters, preparing them for emergencies and things like that."

Nasuh had created a massive organization with sixteen thousand volunteers. They worked for free to save people they didn't know in countries they had never been to. He had become an expert in first-response techniques, writing books and giving lectures throughout the world.

Nasuh sat back, sipping his tea as he explained, "We work with many large companies to support our cause, but we always need equipment. We need vehicles; we need petrol. It costs a lot of money."

As Nasuh told me about his mission, I realized that as much as my trip had recently been teaching me a lot about the past, Nasuh was showing me what I hoped to be my future.

Like with Willy in Colorado, Bekim in Montenegro, Anna in Greece, I knew that I was sitting across from a friend. I shared with him, "A wise man once said to me that one of the greatest sins is to live an unlived life; you, my friend, are living a full life."

"That's what I want to do always," he replied. He thought about it for a moment, putting down his tea as he continued. "I always say to the young people, 'You're not here to make your mother's and father's dreams come true. You're here for your own dreams — to just follow your heart, do what you want. Just go deep inside, into yourself, get to know yourself better, and follow your own path. Because you have your own path behind you, and you have your own path in the future.' We all have the good and bad of humanity within ourselves, and it's up to us which one we let out."

As I was listening to him, I remembered Che's story. For one magical year, Che rode around South America, meeting its people and seeing in them their ultimate goodness. What he found was that men are rarely born evil. More often, they are born hungry. They aren't able to go out and live their dreams because they are too busy fighting for food.

I knew I wanted to be a part of Nasuh's work. I wanted to be a part of giving — both in small ways and also in big ones. I wanted to help him dig down into the chaos and offer people a second chance at life.

"I hope you accept this," I began. "I want to equip twenty-five of your volunteers who go out and save lives in disasters."

Nasuh looked at me, something deep inside of him speaking to something deep inside of me. Because ultimately the gifts weren't just about the monetary offer or even their intended consequences, they carried a message and it said, "I believe in what you do. I support your dream. I connect with who you are."

Nasuh began to nod slowly. His voice

quiet as he replied, "You left your home to find kindness, no? And you meet the world and give kindness. Loving people changes all of us, Leon. Be prepared to change."

The next morning, I had breakfast with Mehmet, and talked about his cousin's work. Mehmet also worked with Nasuh and respected his cousin — not just because they were family, but because he had learned from him just how much good could be done in this world. I thanked Mehmet for his kindness and that of his cousin.

"I feel very fortunate to have bumped into you, and I feel very fortunate that you introduced me to your cousin and that we had the chance to meet," I told him. "I hope you know — I hope you both know — that our friendship doesn't end here."

"Of course not, Leon," Mehmet laughed. "You have family now in Turkey, too. If you need anything, anything at all, you promise me, you let me know. We are now the same, we are, uh, we are like brothers."

As I drove off on Kindness One, I kind of felt like Odysseus setting sail once again. I realized that it was so easy for me to connect to these friends I had met along the way. After one day, it was like I had known them forever. But what about the people I *had* known forever? Could I stay connected once I was home? Or was Lina right? Was I just running from relationships that felt the most permanent?

CHAPTER SEVEN

"What this world needs is a new kind of
army — the army of the kind."
— Cleveland Amory

I lay down in the back of the Bulgarian
truck driver's cab — or what Mihali called
"home" — trying to find a comfortable
position to sleep. I had met Mihali at a truck
stop, and he had offered me a place to stay
for the night, in the not-so-large bed of the
truck that he used to transport lumber
across Europe.

Mihali had kindly cooked me dinner and
given me a place to rest, even if it was next
to a large, snoring Bulgarian. But more than
that, Mihali had offered me the opportunity
to make an important detour on my journey.

We had been having tea before retiring to
his truck, when he told me about the city of
Ephesus: "It is most beautiful city, friend.
City of all faiths. You will be different man

for visit city."

I had become fluent by now in broken English, and from Mihali's description, it sounded like a trip to Ephesus would be a perfect farewell to Turkey. Even though it was a few hundred miles off course.

The ancient city of Ephesus is located in southern Turkey and was once home to the apostle Paul. Historians believe that most of his writings, including those that later became the book of Acts in the New Testament, were written in Ephesus. It wasn't just the religious story that appealed to me, however. As Mihali spoke, I thought back to when I was very young and learned the stories of Paul and the Apostles in Sunday school. I still remembered those words from Paul: "So these three things remain: faith, hope, and love. But the greatest of these is love."

In many ways, it was that sentiment that was driving me east through the ancient lands of our ancestors — Christian, Muslim, Jewish — to experience the birthplaces of so many of the world's major religions. I wouldn't call myself a religious man, but I have come to believe in spirit, and I believe that spirit is often communicated through the mouths of men and women, of people moved by a desire to touch others, to

164

remind us that we are whole and loved.

As Mihali had explained over tea, "Yes, friend. Ephesus very beautiful city, but more beautiful, Ephesus is city of God."

How could I say no to the City of God?

In the morning, I siphoned off some gas from Mihali's stash (with his permission, of course) and was on my way to Ephesus. Several hours later, I walked up to the ancient site where Paul himself once stood, where he shared his experience of Christ with the ancient Greeks who once inhabited this land. But as I quickly found out, if I wanted to see the UNESCO World Heritage Site of Ephesus, I needed more than faith, hope, and love. I also needed cash. All four quickly arrived in the form of a Dutch couple who offered to buy my ticket. I would like to say I convinced them, but I believe it was another case of the charm of Kindness One.

The temple of Artemis was a renowned structure even before Paul arrived to preach the Gospel of Christ. Standing there, I was truly taken aback by the grandeur of this historical marvel built over two thousand years ago. I walked through the broken ruins, and I could feel again those lives that had passed through it. So many lives. So many stories. So many wonderful acts of goodness and hope, pain and betrayal. And in that moment, it was as though history had stopped, as though past and present were one and the same. We have been here for so long, I thought, and yet we barely get the chance to be here at all. In a matter of years, I would no longer be walking through this world. Someone else's footsteps would replace mine, just as I now walked in those of others.

I stepped into the old library, where Paul himself once sat, writing the letters that would later become Acts. I breathed in the musty air, feeling connected to this spirit from long ago. As I imagined Paul writing those words — "But the greatest of these is love" — I could feel his footprints below mine, two thousand years later, his words still lingering amid the ruins.

I continued my tour and ended up at the amphitheater where Paul gave his sermons of peace and kindness, and where he was eventually arrested and sentenced to death. He later escaped the city of Ephesus, which he had made his home and the center of his congregation.

Ultimately it was Paul's message of love that led him to be punished by the powerful Ephesians. That message had earned him many enemies. Throughout history, too many people have been killed because they rankled the powerful by asking that we love one another. But for most of us, love is all any of us really has. It is our source of nourishment and our source of energy. It warms us when the nights grow cold, and when we are faced with fear. When we are walking into territories unknown, it is what connects us to each other, despite which nation we might call home, despite which religion we practice or which beliefs we hold dear.

After leaving the ruins of Ephesus I walked around town and was met with the kindness and generosity that seemed to flow from the Turkish people. Not that I didn't suffer *any* rejection, but it didn't take me long to meet Menekse, a local woman who invited me to have dinner with her and her husband.

It is amazing how modern culture has come to unite us. Even in a small town in Turkey, Menekse wore American blue jeans and an Abercrombie & Fitch T-shirt. First, we went to a local tea shop, where a group of older men sat and smoked hookahs, while younger men and women worked on their laptops or texted on their phones.

As we waited for her husband, I told Menekse where I was off to next, explaining that I had all my visas in place for Iran and Pakistan.

She interrupted me, "You're going to go on your bike?"

"Yes," I answered rather sheepishly, seeing the concern on her face.

She took her cup of tea in hand, "I don't think it's secure going by bike at the moment . . . to those places."

Menekse paused for a moment, as though deciding how best to word her thoughts, "It was a bit warm last month . . . over there."

Before I left on my journey, I had plotted my route, deciding which countries I would see, acquiring the necessary visas, and determining which would be the fastest route across the world. That route included passing through Iran and right into Pakistan. Bold, yes. Daring, sure. But impossible? I really didn't think that would be the case. I had Kindness One to keep me safe and the kind of confidence that fuels such dreams. I imagined driving through Tehran and finding an Islamic family to guide me. I thought I would surely meet some young Pakistanis who would trade a ride on Kindness One for dinner and perhaps a night's stay. I had been dreaming of this part of my trip since I first drew the line from Turkey to India, knowing that this was not only the fastest route, but also the most interesting one.

I knew the trip was risky, but I also knew that this was what this journey was all about — it was about reaching out to people in even the harshest environments and discovering that beneath the politics of more powerful men, we all share the same simple dream: to be happy.

But as Menekse lowered her voice to speak about Iran, as though to even discuss it was dangerous, I wondered if I was being foolish to think I could brazenly ride through the same country on a bright yellow motorbike. But then again, people had warned me about Pittsburgh; they had said to stay out of Kosovo; they had even advised me against Turkey, and I had been blessed by all those experiences.

"How warm is warm?" I asked.

"It's hot," Menekse finally admitted. "It's hot about the war."

As Meneske continued, I could feel my own internal danger meter rising. Though I wasn't sure which war she was referring to, it could have been the troubles in Iraq or the ongoing fight against the Taliban in Afghanistan. She could have been referring to the civil war in Syria or the general unrest of every country I planned on visiting.

"Maybe you change your route?" Menekse asked.

Change my route? I was planning to leave for my route in the morning. I hoped that when Menekse's husband arrived, he might have a more congenial view.

"I think it's not a good idea," Talat offered.

"Not a good idea?" I asked again, hoping for a different response.

"Not a good idea."

Together, Talat, Menekse, and I walked to their home, where I watched the news for the first time in months and saw what all the fuss was really about. Things were getting worse in Syria and throughout the Middle East — no one knew where the violence might strike next. War wasn't just coming. War was *here*. Kindness One doesn't do very well in war. I don't do well in war. The truth is, no one does well in war.

Talat asked me if there was anyone who might be able to get me a plane ticket. That would be great, I explained, but I wasn't sure how I was going to get Kindness One into economy. First class, maybe.

Then I remembered that Mehmet had told me that if I ever needed any help I should call him. Could this be a moment to reach out my hand and ask for assistance? I knew that if anyone would understand my predicament it would be Mehmet and Nasuh. I also knew that if anyone could help me circumnavigate an entire region of the world, it would be my new Turkish family.

I called Mehmet to see if he could help.

Mehmet was happy to hear from me, but I wasn't sure for how long as I explained my predicament, and asked his advice: "I've met a lot of people and I've told them I'm traveling east through Iran and Pakistan. And the reaction I've received has been pretty bad."

Mehmet replied with a thoughtful: "Mm, hmm."

It wasn't the reaction I was hoping for, but I continued, "I mean, evidently something is happening in the Middle East that suggests that going through those two countries is not very wise right now. So I just wanted to know what you thought about that. If there was another solution."

Silence.

Bad news typically follows silence.

I don't like silence.

Or bad news for that matter.

"Look Leon, I thought about it when you told me in Istanbul," Mehmet replied, his voice deep and serious. "Maybe this route is not such a good idea, but every day it's looking worse. I think your friends there are right. You should not continue."

Should not continue? I felt my rebellious side surge up, wanting to respond to Mehmet's warning with, "Not continue? Are you mad? The Ambassador of Kindness is not stopped by war. The Ambassador of Kindness —"

Who the hell was I kidding? The Ambassador of Kindness didn't like the idea of driving through or *near* a war either, but I still had a worldwide quest to complete. I tried to explain, "Not continuing isn't really an option, my friend. Either I find another way around, or I have to go through."

"Hmmm," Mehmet replied. I liked the sound of that. Thinking is better than silence. Mehmet told me he would call me back. He might have a plan. Plans are good, especially ones that don't involve war.

After eating dinner with Talat and Menekse, I received the call.

"Leon," Mehmet began, his voice brimming with joy. "Pack your bags, we have found you a plane."

I didn't know what to say. A plane was great, but what about Kindness One?

But then Mehmet corrected himself, "A cargo plane."

Could this moment even be happening? Here I was in a small Turkish town, threatened by a Middle Eastern war directly in my path, eating dinner at the home of a kind and concerned couple I had just met on the street, a couple who might have just saved my life, and Kindness One was being offered a trip to India via cargo plane.

"You will have to come back to Istanbul," Mehmet explained. "But then you will go to India."

I couldn't thank Mehmet enough, but I still had a decision to make.

Thankfully, Talat and Menekse had the Internet. And Lina and I had Skype. In most of the places I had stayed, I didn't have good enough service to actually see her, but now across the miles, her warm face came into grainy view.

"Good morning, Penelope," I said, though she had no idea what I was talking about.

I explained my situation.

She sighed. It was the kind of sigh that said, *Really, Leon, is this even a question?*

"I mean, we kind of knew this was going to be an issue," she reminded me.

"Yeah," I agreed. "But I *hoped* it wouldn't be an issue."

"You hope too much," she replied, her voice tired.

"I miss you, Lina," I said, hoping those words might encapsulate everything I felt in that moment — my fears, my excitement, and the distance that even Skype was unable to bridge.

"I miss you, too," the video began to break up, but I still heard Lina's words. "You don't need to come home now, Leon, but you need to come home safe."

I could barely see her face anymore, as the image froze and rearranged itself.

I nodded, not knowing if she could still hear me.

"I'll be home soon," were my last words before the connection was lost altogether.

Talat and Menekse showed me to my own bed. After spending the previous night listening to the heavy snores of a Bulgarian truck driver, I finally got to do something I had been dreaming about all day: sleep.

When I woke up in the morning, my decision had been made. I knew that dreams could be fickle — sometimes they had to change in order to be achieved. Perhaps Mihali's suggested detour had done more than introduce me to Ephesus — it might have just saved my life.

I said my good-byes to Talat and Menekse, and thanked them for their gentle nudging. I am sure that Lina would have thanked them as well. Menekse looked at me and smiled. I could see relief on her face, but also surprise. I don't even think she could quite believe what had just happened.

And here again, goodness and darkness found themselves overlapping. The generosity of my friends in Turkey standing in contrast to the war that was exploding all around them. And those friends who had suddenly popped up across the landscape all echoed my greatest friend back home — make it home safe.

Often, it just takes a little bit of faith, hope, and love, for us to see that a broken plan doesn't mean a broken dream. It just means another path will open up.

I arrived in Istanbul and went straight to the airport, meeting up with Mehmet's contact to begin the arrangements for the plane and to have the bike crated and expedited to its new destination: India! I sat in my seat — a far cry from first class, but far safer than riding Kindness One across Iran. I looked down at the world below. If flowers can grow through concrete, love can surely sprout in violence. There was no way to keep it down. Because "these three things remain: faith, hope, and love," and Paul was right: The greatest of these is love.

· · · ·

Ever since I was a child, I had dreamed of seeing India. It was probably all those Rudyard Kipling stories, which made me think it was filled with elephants and monkeys and boys raised in the wild. But as I grew older, the dream changed. I no longer imagined that I would be running through the jungle next to a tiger. I dreamed that I would be riding through it on a motorbike. I thought that in India I might meet God.

On my arrival in Delhi, the first thing that hit me was the heat. Humid. Powerful. Overwhelming, 120-degree heat. The second thing: the poverty. It was gut-wrenching poverty, the type where emaciated children begged with dirty fingers and whole families slept in the streets, in homes made out of cardboard.

As I stepped out of the airport, I thought I would be confronted with color and spice, and instead I was hit with unspeakable sadness. How was it possible that so many could have so little?

Once I got into the city, I parked Kindness One and began to explore on foot. Children cried out to me, "Meester! Meester!" hoping to get just a rupee from me. For the first time on this trip, I was embarrassed to be without money. Sure, I had seen homeless people in Turkey, in Greece, in America, but nothing like this. How could I come to India with no money to give? How could I ask its people for help when I should be the one offering it?

I turned down a quiet street and away from the busy road filled with honking buses and scooters. The sidewalk had been turned to rubble by the trees growing underneath, the roots breaking up the concrete, making an uneven path down the narrow street.

I saw three "Westerners" (which I quickly found out was the word used for all white people in India) standing outside a building. I walked up only to discover it was an ashram.

I went inside and saw a handful of people meditating in a garden, lush green foliage hanging down over them as they sat in silence.

Off to the side was a small bookstore, which appeared open. A bookstore? Why not?

Inside, there was an older man with a long white beard sitting at the register. He was reading a book with an even older man on its cover.

He looked up at me and asked quietly, "How can I help you, son?"

I breathed a sigh of relief. After feeling powerless to help anyone outside this quiet sanctuary, I was so grateful to feel that there was someone I could share this burden with. I told him everything about my journey around the world on kindness, about all the ups and all the downs. I told him that though I intended to offer people gifts along the way, I didn't know what to do about asking his people for help. How could I do that? How could I come here with empty pockets?

He lay down his book and smiled, "My child, money is not inside the pocket. Many Indians have no pockets and no money. But what do they have is biggest hearts. Remember that God is inside us all. A man will only help you if he can. And if he cannot, he will not help. This is not your concern. Let it be."

I felt in awe of this man. He had calmed my spirit, *and* he had quoted The Beatles.

I thanked him profusely.

"If there was something I could give the ashram, I would . . ." I began, but he shook his head.

"You can go meet India. Love her. That will be your gift."

I walked back out onto the street, my faith restored. And you know what happened next? Nothing. Well nothing good anyway. First, I stepped in cow shit. Yes you heard that right, literally two minutes after I left the holy man, I stepped in cow shit. Second, no one would help me. No one. In fact they all wanted *my* help. Third, I was beginning to think that the man who I had spoken to only forty-five minutes earlier might have actually been a mirage brought on by the stifling heat.

I was about to give up hope when I bumped into a chap standing ncxt to a motorcycle rickshaw. Dheeru was well dressed and spoke only broken English, but we were still able to understand one another.

I told him of my journey, "I left Los Angeles in America, and I got all the way to Delhi completely on the kindness of other people."

At first, I wasn't sure how much he understood me, but then a big smile broke out across his face, "That's my culture!"

He wobbled his head back and forth, which I quickly learned was a common Indian gesture, meaning that the person heard what you were saying, even if they weren't sure they knew how to respond.

Dheeru continued, "My culture is kind and respectable. Everybody is like a guest who comes in."

After a few more minutes of chatting, I decided this was the type of man my holy friend was pointing me toward. But then I remembered that after leaving him, I had stepped in cow shit. So I asked my standard question with a bit of trepidation, "Is there any way that today I could stay in your house?"

"My house?" he responded, looking very confused. The kind of confused that says, "Why does this white man with a yellow motorbike want to stay in my house?"

"Yes," I replied.

But then Dheeru's eyes opened wide and he wobbled his head, replying, "Yes, you could stay in my house. My place has a lot of people living in it."

Long live Indian rickshaw drivers! Long live Dheeru!

That day was a holiday in India, and thus the streets were somewhat empty (which made me wonder what they might look like full). Dheeru had far fewer customers than usual, so he offered to take me back to his home to meet his family. I had been fore-warned never to go to the slums of India. I had heard stories of people being robbed, beaten, some even killed. I had been told that Westerners do not go to the slums. Well, this Westerner had heeded enough warnings for one trip. I felt safe in Dheeru's presence, and I remembered the old man's words at the ashram, "Meet India. Love her. That will be your gift."

Dheeru drove me in his rickshaw to the slum where he and his wife and two sons lived in a one-room shack. In one bed.

His wife brewed us some chai as we went outside and he told me about their life. We sat in lawn chairs that could have once been in the backyard of any American home.

I asked Dheeru, "So you've told me how hard it is to make a living in India. How much do you make a week, if you don't mind me asking?"

He looked at his wife as she came outside with the tea. Wobbling his head before replying, "Rickshaw is very hard. If don't get customers for two, three days, no eat."

"So sometimes you and your family do not eat for two or three days?" I asked, overwhelmed at the thought that his whole family would go hungry.

"Yes," Dheeru explained, as though it was the simplest fact. "It depends on my work. If I work, we eat . . ."

I found it heartbreaking that they sometimes went without food. How could there be a world with so much and yet another world with so little?

We sat and talked about life and love. He told me he had always dreamed of being a rickshaw driver, though he still hoped that one day he would own his own.

"What does that mean?" I asked him. "Do you pay someone else?"

"Oh, yes," Dheeru laughed. "I pay much to drive rickshaw."

Rent was not cheap for rickshaws, I learned. Whatever money Dheeru had left over he spent on his family, but often there was not much. He had no money for his sons to attend secondary school. He had no savings should his wife get sick, or worse, if something should happen to him. They lived one inch from disaster in a one-room shack, and yet as he explained, they still gave to those who had even less. Just as I had seen in Pittsburgh, in Turkey, in France, there were so many people who survived by their connections to other people. They were creating a web of kindness, taking care of each other, and being taken care of in turn.

As Dheeru told me, the little money his family had left over went to others, "When there is good day, when we have some more, we give to orphans."

"What?" I asked, thinking I had misheard him at first.

"That's Indian culture," he replied. "If I have a nice client give lots of money, I give to orphanage. You know, children that don't have mums and dads."

By now, a crowd had gathered outside, word spreading through the community that a Westerner had come to visit Dheeru and his family. I had become a celebrity — and I didn't even have Kindness One with me! As Dheeru took me on a walk through the slum, a group of children followed at a close distance, giggling and whispering as though I were the King of England. Just as I had grown up on stories of India, so they had grown up on stories of Britain.

I looked around at the women sitting outside, the men coming home from work, the children behind us, and immediately saw the paradox: Though there was extreme poverty, there was also extreme joy. Of course, there is no greater pain than a hungry belly, and living a spiritual life also requires having one's physical needs met, but I also saw that in the absence of material things, the bonds of family and the camaraderie of friendship were not just about friendly social connection. They were about survival. They were about love. They were one home connecting to another home, lighting up the grid of this world.

I wished I could do something that would change all of their lives for the better, but I knew that I did have the power to change one life, and in that transformation, I hoped that many more might be touched.

When Dheeru and I returned to his home, I asked him, "What about renting your rickshaw? How much is that a day?"

"Rickshaw rent is 300 rupees a day," he replied. I quickly did the math and realized that was about $10 a day. Dheeru thought about it and added, "And uh, 200 rupees for the fuel."

"So it costs you 500 rupees a day?" I confirmed with him.

He wobbled his head, making me wonder whether it was a yes or a no, but then he explained, "After 500 rupees, I make goes in my pocket."

"So how much do you make on average?" I probed.

"On average, 800 rupees, but then I pay owner of rickshaw."

"And the fuel," I finished his sentence.

There was so little left for them and yet here they were, cooking me dinner, offering me one of their few mats to sleep on. Inviting me into the web of kindness.

Later, as I lay my head down to sleep in one of the poorest parts of the world, I felt a richness pervade my soul. India had not been what I dreamed it would be, but sometimes our dreams are limiting. Who needs tigers when you have love?

As the sun rose on the slums of this small part of India, I convened an impromptu family meeting, during which I planned to let Dheeru and his family in on my secret. "You see," I explained. "This journey is all about kindness. It's all about the generosity of the human spirit. That's why I started this journey, and that's why I find myself here with you. Having spent the night in your home, having spent the night with your whole family, I feel very, very welcome. And for that, I am truly grateful."

"This is our culture," explained Dheeru. "You are now part of our family."

He reached out and grabbed hold of my hand, and I felt it. I was a part of his family, just as he had quickly become a part of mine, joining Willy and Tony and Anna and Mehmet in the growing group of brothers and sisters who had become the heart of this journey. In many ways, I was a boy raised in the wild. I didn't understand the ways of those around me, and I always felt like I didn't belong in the concrete jungle of money and business deals and exceedingly good manners. Maybe a part of me belonged in India, long before I ever had the chance to meet her. I wobbled my head back at Dheeru, not even realizing I had already picked up the habit.

I continued on, preparing them for what I hoped would be the gift to change their lives: "You told me that sometimes you don't have enough money to feed your family and that sometimes your children go hungry for days. And you told me you were a hero in Indian culture because you had the rickshaw. Well . . . I want to buy you a new rickshaw."

I want to buy you a new rickshaw? I never thought I would utter those words. And I never thought they would mean so much when I did.

Evidently, Dheeru never expected to hear them. He was totally stunned. He couldn't quite believe this was happening.

"Is it possible?" he whispered.

"Absolutely," I replied, a wide smile now breaking across my face. "I am going to buy you your own rickshaw."

"If it's very possible, I'm very, very happy for you to," Dheeru stuttered, his excitement making his English even more broken. "Because I work like this. I want this change for my family and change of my living status, you know. So everybody's looking for this dream, and if it is possible, I am so happy."

"It is very possible," I reiterated.

After a long pause he replied, "How can I thank you? I don't know how I'm going to thank you. I am very happy, very happy. I am . . . I don't know."

And then that smile returned. I would have given Dheeru everything I owned for that smile. It was one of joy; it was one of love; and it was, despite their poverty and struggles, one of utter contentment.

Once I was able to convince him that he was not dreaming and that he really would be receiving his very own rickshaw, we sat down for breakfast with his wife and sons.

As we ate, Dheeru started realizing what the rickshaw would mean. "It will change everything," he explained. He looked at his sons, "Life, education. I can give a good education for a long time for my children. I can extend to go to a nice house, good education, and good place for life."

Dheeru and his family deserved a good place to live. They deserved good lives. I left the slum that morning and walked back to where I had parked Kindness One the day before. I thought of my own family back at home — Lina and Winston. We had so much — a wonderful house, the knowledge that we would never go hungry — and yet I often failed to appreciate the most important part of our life: We had love.

I revved up Kindness One and heard a little cough in her start. I hoped it wasn't anything. I couldn't imagine trying to fix the motorbike along the crazy roads of India, but I knew it was like the old man in the ashram said: "Let it be."

Kindness One and me on the road, ready for adventure.

Sleeping on the rough streets of Pittsburgh with my new friend, Tony.

The moment Tony realized that he was no longer homeless . . .

Couldn't resist the "I'm the king of the world moment" on my voyage across the Atlantic.

Making new friends at a barbecue during my Atlantic crossing.

Fencing in the streets of Trieste with Alex, the man who offered to give his gift to someone more needy.

My friend Alex and his protégé, Angelo, with the gift of new fencing equipment.

The Montenegrin farmer, Bekim, and his family with their new cow!

Overwhelmed with love in a rural Indian village.

Broken down on the streets of Patna.

My Indian friend Dheeru and his family next to their new rickshaw.

(*Opposite*) Sitting all alone amidst the majestic beauty of the Taj Mahal in India.

Paying my respects at the tomb of Mother Theresa in Calcutta.

Meditating in Bhutan at the biggest statue of Buddha in the world.

Kids at the Calcutta orphanage drinking clean water for the first time.

The infamous Killing Tree in Cambodia.

Seng and Mai in their new house.

A group of rural Vietnamese after their successful eye surgeries.

Performing at the opera house in Ho Chi Minh City.

Almost home . . .

CHAPTER EIGHT

"If there were no schools to take the
children away from home part of the time,
the insane asylums would be filled
with mothers."
— Edgar W. Howe

I have a confession to make, admittedly it is
over twenty years late, but as they say, better late than never: I hated school. Almost
every minute I was forced to sit at that desk,
listening to teachers, was pure, unadulter-
ated hell. And I had the grades to prove it.
At one point, I scored 18% on a chemistry
exam. And the fact that I got 18% of the
questions correct was a near miracle. No,
unfortunately, memorizing facts and being
tested on them was just two rungs up from
Chinese water torture. I didn't realize it
until much later, but the reason for that was
that facts and figures and chemistry didn't
speak to me. Other people's stories did.

Although my schooling wasn't much of a success, I found another way of learning. It was by fantasizing about walking on the moon that I became interested in astronomy. It was by wondering where the hell Antarctica was that I pulled out my first map. It was by dreaming that I would ride a motorcycle across the world that one day . . . Well, you know the rest.

And yet without the education I received, I don't know that I would have ever been open to those lessons. It was because I understood the context of the countries that I was visiting, that I was also better able to understand their people . . . and ultimately myself. I walked through India with my English accent, keenly aware of the role my country had played in the history of this modern nation. I quickly saw how my Queen's English and my white skin affected the dynamics between me and the people I met. I could feel the weight of history as though it were riding next to me in Kindness One's sidecar. But I knew that in dropping the mask, the mask of my accent, and that of the horrendous baggage of our mutual past, that in some way, the dynamic might be shifted yet again.

No school could teach the lessons of India. It seemed that all the crises of the world — poverty, inequality, spirituality, and a glut of technology — were playing out on the broken rubble of its streets. And perhaps this was no more true than in Delhi, where the modern world sat right on top of the ancient one, the old roots of Hinduism and Islam rising through the billboard ads for cell phones and Coca-Cola.

As I had anticipated, it was difficult to find people to give me things they did not have. I spent nearly an entire day sitting at a gas station waiting for someone to give me gas. Apparently (like the sport of cricket), waiting was a national pastime in India, and I was becoming quite accomplished in it. But what I received in place of gas or water or even food were the stories of a nation. People were always willing to stop and talk, despite the language barriers and my awkward explanation of how I, a white man in India, had no money.

Finally, I met someone who was able to help, offering me a tank of gas and my first meal of the day before I got on the road again, off to the Taj Mahal. The Taj Mahal was famously built by the Shah Jahan in the 1600s in honor of his wife, who died in childbirth. It is a testament to their love, and the loss that only such a love can bring. It took twenty years and over twenty thousand workers to build it. It is rumored that when it was done, the Shah had the main architect killed so that no copy of it could be completed elsewhere. And when you stand before it, you can't help but understand, just a little bit, why.

Two young Dutch girls had taken pity on me and paid for my entrance to the site. While walking the marble halls, I looked around, and it seemed like the entire site was filled with couples holding hands. Suddenly I felt terribly alone, as though I had no one else to talk to, and never would again. I had no one to share this with. I remembered Lina's face on my computer, and suddenly Los Angeles seemed a long, long way away. Antarctica felt closer. But that's probably because it was!

I left the Taj with a heavy heart, which may or may not have been the cause of the following incident. Now when I took my driving test in London, which I passed on the sixth attempt, one of the things I was taught was to stay *on* the road. I swear, I was never told by any driving instructor, ever, that I should drive *off* the road and into a wall. But what can I say? I'm a rule breaker. And apparently, a wall breaker, because only half a mile away from the Shah's testament to the eternity of love, I rode my motorbike right into a wall. A hard wall. A freshly painted hard wall. The only one in India I believe.

Once I shook off the shock of the collision — where did that wall come from, anyway? — I realized a few things: one, that I wasn't hurt; two, that no one else was involved; three, that the wall had taken a big chunk out of my precious yellow bike; and four, that Kindness One wouldn't start.

When I looked underneath the engine, I saw that there was a dreaded leak. I had not only failed my chemistry test and my driving exam, but I was also clearly failing the course on motorbike management that I had inadvertently signed up for in taking this trip.

For those of you who haven't been to India, I am about to share one of its many secrets: When anything goes wrong in India, people arrive. Lots of people. They mingle. They watch. They chatter among themselves. They often try and help. When an Englishman on a yellow motorbike drives into a freshly painted wall, the whole town comes out. Including, as I found out, the local karate master.

I am not joking. I mean at the moment, I wondered whether I was seeing things, but that's an upside of having a camera crew with you. They can help you identify the difference between crazy shit that actually happened and good old-fashioned hallucinations, and the karate master was no hallucination.

After introducing himself in broken English, which was much better than my Hindi, I asked him, "What color belt do you have?"

"Black belt," he replied dryly as he walked around my bike. I had managed to stop the leak, but Kindness One was going to need a lot more help than that.

"Can you teach me some karate?" I asked, thinking this would lighten the mood a bit, and maybe convince the karate teacher to help a fellow out.

"Done. And change to uniform."

I know, I know. This moment can't be real. There is no way a karate master stopped to look at my bike and brought along with him a freshly cleaned karate costume in my size. Well, that first part is all true. The size part — not so much. The jacket fit tightly over my T-shirt, and the pants barely fit around my trousers, but it was good enough for the karate master and certainly for the quickly growing audience around us.

Our first interactions were quite gentle,

but then the karate master stood back and smiled.

"I will hug you," he stated for all to hear. I was ready to be embraced, thinking our lesson was over. I should have paid more attention to my karate instructor when I was young. Never expect a hug.

Instead, what I got was a jarring kick to the face. As though riding my bike into a wall hadn't been bad enough, I had also just ridden my face into this stranger's foot. He started to circle me, showing off some Bollywood moves for the audience as they laughed and cheered him on. What had I gotten myself into? I was about to get my arse kicked less than a mile away from the international epicenter of love. I guess in India "I will hug you" actually means "I will kick you in the face until you beg for mercy."

So that's what I did. On my knees. And then I tried to run away. Finally, I found a translator from the crowd who told the master that I didn't actually know karate. Finally, he understood. I was looking for a teacher. He thought he had found a sparring partner.

After I spent the better part of ten minutes prostrate on the ground, the karate teacher finally offered me a hand of friendship. Rajat had not only stopped trying to beat me up, but also asked if I needed a place to stay for the night. It seemed I had earned his kindness through my lack of karate skills. I was just grateful I didn't have to go through that every time I asked someone for help.

We walked Kindness One back to his small two-room house in a shanty town not far from the Taj. There, I was able to keep an eye on the leaking situation. Rajat told me to calm down and that in the morning he would send me to one of his friends who would fix the leak. Of course, this was coming from a man who had kicked me in the face only hours before. As I lay down on the mat Rajat had offered me, I thought again of Lina. I don't know why I find relationships to be so much harder when I'm in them. From here, in India, Lina and our home sounded like the best place on earth. And yet, I had learned over the years that, once I settled back home, I always felt the need to go again. I wondered whether it was like being in school. I liked the idea of it, but the reality always made me feel like the walls were closing in on me.

When I woke up in the morning, Agra looked different in the dawn's light — kinder, gentler. Rajat sent me to a local mechanic who patched up the leak for free.

I started up Kindness One and was ready again to hit the open roads of India.

Or shall I say the *broken* roads of India? How do I put this tactfully? How about this? The Indian roads are a complete death trap. Hell waits for you at every corner. Cars drive right at you. Cows pop out of nowhere. Children play in the middle of the road. There are no rules. Precious little asphalt. No trustworthy stoplights or speed limits. There is nothing but absolute, astonishing fear. If you ever have the chance to drive in India. Don't. Just. Don't. You have been warned.

I had decided to ride to Lucknow, which is a big town in the center of India, and from the sound of it, a great place to get some luck, now. My bike, however, had other plans. While on the road to fortune, Kindness One started spluttering and then stopped in the middle of a highway. The truck drivers weren't happy. The cows weren't happy. Kindness One wasn't happy. And I won't even tell you how I was feeling. But it had been during moments like this that I had often witnessed people at their kindest. They could smell the desperation or see the exhaustion or know, because they had been there many times themselves, when someone just needed some help.

The sun was fading, and things were looking bad, but I was in luck now without even having made it to the aforementioned city yet. Although I had stopped in the middle of the street, I had also stopped right next to a roadside pancake seller. He and his nine children, ranging in age from four to sixteen, helped push my bike to the corner and let me stay the night with them. If you think that sleeping on a straw mattress under the stars is a good night's sleep, well it is. It was a perfect night of sleep. In the morning, the family even patched up my bike and gave me gas. As I was quickly learning, there was probably no better place in the world for a bike to break down than in India. Because nearly everyone rode them, and unlike you-know-who, they all knew how to fix them. Incredible India indeed!

I arrived in Lucknow only to find that, once again, a white man with a British accent was cause for curiosity but not generosity. And again, I understood. Even I was embarrassed for the chap. I did my best not to get run over by the Lucknow traffic as I made my way to an outdoor teashop. It was one of many that lined the streets of India. Old men selling chai to a short but steady line. I began to talk with a man while he waited for his tea, hoping he might buy me one, too.

"Is it normally this hot in India?" I asked, getting used to striking up conversations with strangers.

"Yes. Now it's cool. You can say it's cool."

"It's cool?" I responded. "Cool is 60 degrees. Not 110!"

"I'd even say it's cold," the man said laughing. Ajay was in his early twenties and looked as though he might work for a tech company or ride a motorbike of his own. He replied in near-perfect English, "It's much more hot in the summers."

"I think I've lost about fifteen kilos of body weight already . . ."

"That means you were huge!" he laughed again, and I knew that I was making a friend. I explained to him my journey and also my hunger, hoping that he wouldn't dismiss me as so many had already done that day.

Ajay countered with my favorite reply, "You're looking for a place to stay the night?"

This man was good.

"Yes, I am," I replied, trying not to appear too desperate. Finally, my luck was looking up.

"So, I don't have a place to stay for you," Ajay began. "But I'm going to the bus station on the way to my village. If you like, I can take you there, and you can stay there."

"How far away is your village?" I asked.

"From Lucknow, it's a hundred kilometers. I can take you there, and you can see new things, and they will show you kindness. If you want to come with me, I will take you on a safe journey, and I can buy you a bus ticket to it."

I explained that I had my motorbike and offered to give him a ride if he could take care of the gas. He gladly agreed, and added lunch into the deal as well.

A good friend once told me, "Don't quit before the miracle happens." I had applied those words to my career, to my relationships, to my life choices, but I had begun to realize that nowhere did they apply more than in India. The miracles were there, hidden beneath the thick smog, the piles of trash alongside the road, the hurried and desperate pace of its people. You just had to be willing to wait, and sometimes you had to wait a really long time (like, a really, really long time), but somewhere in that mess of smells and people and color, miracles occurred.

As Ajay and I drove into the village, I realized my new friend had evidently called in advance, telling his friends and family of my impending arrival. The whole village had come out to welcome me. All of them. Even the cows.

I felt like a Bollywood star coming back to his hometown for a visit. During our short drive there, a whole show had been put together in my honor. There were singers. And dancers. And cows. And children, lots and lots of children.

Everyone in the village seemed to own a cell phone, and they were all taking photos and videos of our entrance. It appeared that the digital revolution had reached the backwaters of India, but white men on yellow motorbikes had not.

Music seemed to fill the air. I wasn't even sure where it was coming from, but as the children and the people from the village danced around me, I felt myself join in. Almost instantly, it was as though we were one moving body, and not separate people. We danced past the small mud huts of the village, moving across the dirt road. I felt myself laughing so hard, I had forgotten about the days of travel, the exhaustion, the fear. I forgot about everything but the present moment, dancing with strangers who without a word had become my friends. For a while, Ajay joined along with us, bouncing up and down next to me, sharing

201

in my laughter, but in the mayhem of people and dancers and cell phones and cows, I lost sight of him.

Thankfully, it didn't take long for me to find him again. After the drive to the village and my impromptu dance performance, I was feeling the exhaustion.

"You are very popular," Ajay laughed.

"It's amazing," I told him. "Your people are amazing. But I don't how much longer I'm going to be able to stand. Never mind dance."

"No problem, no problem," Ajay replied as he led me and the rest of the village to an elder's house, where I could get some rest. Outside the front door, however, hundreds of Indians waited, taking pictures, videos, and singing and dancing. Finally, Ajay was able to convince the crowds that I needed some sleep.

I hadn't slept in a bed in over two days, during which I had run into a wall, been kicked in the face, and had traveled more Indian roads than I would ever want to again, and though I was overwhelmed with the love and attention, I was also, quite frankly, overwhelmed.

The next morning, the village was calmer as Ajay took me around and introduced me to the people who made up his home. So many stories, so many lives, all pulsing together in one common rhythm. When I was a kid, this was the school I had dreamed of attending. There were no facts and figures, no dates and names — just the shared and miraculous human experience of people living and dying and trying to create the best lives they could in the process.

Ajay explained to his neighbors what I was doing and though I knew that my choice to travel with no money confused them — as much as on some days it confused me — they were all excited that I had come to their village.

Ajay laughed, "They think next time you should bring some money."

I agreed with him, "Next time, I will."

As the morning sun began its ascent, the villagers made sure my tank of gas was full and that I had a solid breakfast, and as I rode alone away from my new friends, their love at my back, I knew yet another miracle had arrived.

I had decided that my next stop would be Varanasi, the city of fire, and the holiest city of India. Varanasi is not like New York. It doesn't have skyscrapers. Varanasi is not like Barcelona. It doesn't have a beautiful coastline. Varanasi is not like my hometown of London. It doesn't have tree-lined avenues leading into a lovely inner city park (that's Hyde Park, for those of you who haven't visited). Nestled on the banks of the most famous river in the world, the Ganges, Varanasi is a city of life. But also, it is a city of death.

"Coming to India with yellow bike is much strangeness!" the small man yelled at me as I walked along the Ganges. Not far from where we stood, there was an open fire, and within it, the body of a recently deceased person. No, that was not a typo. A person. A dead person being burned in the open air before their ashes were to be thrown into the Ganges. Hindus believe that if you die and are thrown into the Ganges you will not need to be reincarnated. A goal of all Hindus, I was told.

I thought our proximity to death would warm this stranger's heart, but apparently burning your dead in the open was natural in Varanasi, while riding a yellow motorbike was "much strangeness." It was my final rejection for the day. I had already been through many others as I made my way to this holy town along the banks of the famous Ganges.

I sat down by the river. If Zen is pure mental and physical exhaustion, then I was the living Buddha. I could barely remember my own name, let alone form a coherent thought. All I could do was sit and stare at the river, the smoke, the strange and bewildering world I had found myself in.

An older man walked past and then stopped, asking me what I was doing.

I didn't know how to respond. I was tired of asking for help only to be rejected.

"I don't know," I finally replied, unable to say much more.

"One day you, too, will end up like this," he shared, referring to the fires burning around us. "Live inside this moment and do not lose this time."

He walked away, quickly consumed by the crowds, but his words remained. Those small moments — like the sunset on that Nebraskan farm or playing music with Finesse and Tchale or having tea with my new friend in Turkey — they were immortal. The dead could burn; life could be reborn; but none of it mattered, unless we were willing to live inside the moment.

I stood up. Suddenly, India was not a great heaving beast, but a collection of small steps, of endless stories, of magic amid the mayhem. It was my job to stay in the moment. I continued to walk along the Ganges and soon met Dilip, a young riverboat driver, who offered to take me for a dip in the Ganges. Dilip was short and slim like many Indians, but his arms were bigger than most, built up by his days on the river.

In Greek myth, Charon is the name of the riverboat driver who escorts dead souls across the river Styx to Hades, the kingdom of the dead. I'm not saying Dilip was the Indian understudy for Charon, but as I boarded his boat on the murky Ganges, intending to swim in it, I hoped he wouldn't be leading me to Hades anytime soon.

Because you see, taking a dip in the Ganges is not like taking a dip in the crisp blue waters of Lake Como. Although it is one of the holiest rivers in the world, it is also one of the dirtiest. I had seen numerous dead carcasses floating past me. A dog. Two cows. A few unidentified objects.

They say that in taking a dip in the Ganges you cleanse yourself of all your pain and suffering, but as Dilip and I drove along the dark and dreary water, I asked him: "Have you ever *actually* swum in the Ganges?"

"Yes," he replied, looking out across the water, clearly not feeling the same agitation that I was. I later found out that Dilip was from one of the lower castes in India. Though he wasn't a Dalit — one of the "Untouchables," as they are referred to —

he came low enough on the rung that being a riverboat driver was nearly akin to being a king. He wasn't breaking out of his caste, but he certainly wasn't being defined by it, either. He had chosen a path that few in his family would have ever dared to try.

I continued speaking even if my guide was less talkative, "It's so interesting to me that they use the Ganges for life, they use the Ganges for death . . . it's everything. It's like the circle of life."

When Dilip didn't respond, I confirmed. "Have generations of your family lived and died on the Ganges?"

"Of course," Dilip replied again nonchalantly before looking at me in earnest. "Many people do like this. I am no different."

Dilip pulled the boat over. It was time for us to receive purification and hopefully not a deadly case of typhoid.

"Are you sure this is a wise thing to do?" I asked, finally feeling the fear move through me as we stripped down to our shorts.

"Yes," Dilip responded. "Swimming in the Ganges will purify your karma. Clean the soul."

Dilip offered me a large red scarf to wrap around my waist, which apparently was the proper attire for swimming in the Ganges.

He looked out again over the water, "This is God. By feeling the vibrations, you're always thinking, always changing."

We said a prayer together, and then I stepped apprehensively into the cold water. Dilip moved quickly passed me, submerging himself and splashing the water on his face.

"I'm definitely not going to do that," I thought out loud, not even realizing the words were escaping me.

Dilip laughed, "It's okay, Leon. Many Westerners come swim in the Ganges."

I got in a bit farther as I asked Dilip, "You do this every day?"

He nodded as I pressed forward, "And you don't get sick?"

Dilip shook his head as I asked one more question, "Do you drink the water?"

"Yes," he replied and then he took a drink. Okay, I hate to remind you of this fact, but again, I had just seen numerous dead carcasses float past me. A dog. Two cows. A few unidentified objects.

"Okay," I replied, stepping deeper into the water. "Well, that's not going to happen with me."

Dilip laughed again, "This is probably safer for you."

I looked around. Not far from us, there

was a wedding taking place on a boat. The sun was beginning to settle beneath the famous river as Dilip waded deeper into the water. I looked around, and for a moment, it didn't even feel as though I was on planet Earth. Instead, I was in one of the many stories I had read when I was young.

Because the one thing I do remember from school are the tales of the Greek gods. Maybe it had to do with my own heritage, but as Dilip and I stood in the Ganges, I thought back to all the heroes who had traveled across the river in Charon's boat — Heracles, Orpheus, Dionysus, and of course, Odysseus. They all were returned to the land of the living renewed and wiser for the journey. If they could do it, why couldn't I?

I told Dilip as we bathed in the river, "I started my journey in Los Angeles at the Hollywood sign — the place where capitalism thrives — and here I am in the Ganges, the holiest place for Hindus, with you, someone I have just met."

Dilip stood up and smiled, "Yes because God does good things."

He offered to give me a blessing in the river, speaking the prayer in Hindi and asking me to repeat it. We held hands as we prayed — two men from different sides of the world, with entirely different life experiences, standing together in the Ganges, cleansing our souls. Masks officially dropped.

After we got out of the river, Dilip asked if I wanted to stay with him and his family in their house for the night. We walked back to where he lived with his wife, Dharmin, and their two wonderful sons, Amrit, who was five, and the youngest, Ashish, who was two.

As we ate dinner, Dilip explained that Amrit had been going to school but that they had had to take him out, as they could no longer afford it.

"The school is too much money," Dilip explained. "And sometimes, I do not get enough passengers."

For so many years, I took my education for granted. I hated school, but I could never imagine not having had it. It was there that I fell in love with the stories of history. It was there that I spun my first globe, looking at all the places in the world I hoped to one day see. And though I failed chemistry and algebra and a couple of other classes that we don't need to talk about here, it was at school that I also learned how to meet new people, create friendships, and find my place in the world.

I looked at Amrit and Ashish, and I

couldn't imagine them not having that opportunity. The power of an education, whether it's the traditional kind or one fueled by imagination, could forever alter the course of a life.

At sunset, I took Dilip and his two young sons for a walk along the banks of the Ganges, where I had just swum. Dilip held his younger son in his arms, bouncing him as we walked, showering the boy with affection, the outward proof of love. It was this love that would always keep us alive, long past our actual mortality. It was through our children that we lived beyond our own lifetimes, carrying us into the great beyond. Dilip explained how he wanted his boys to have a better life than he had. He wanted them to have better jobs. A better existence.

"I will do what I can to help them go to school," Dilip shared, his eyes filling with tears of determination. "I teach them."

"You teach them yourself?" I asked.

"Yes, in the night time. I come home, and then I teach them."

In the West, school is open to everyone. We see it as a right, not a privilege. But in India, education comes with school fees, even for those who barely have enough to eat.

"Money's always a problem everywhere,"

Dilip explained. "Who doesn't have money problem?"

He was right. You could ask the richest man in the world if he had a problem with money, and he would say yes. You ask the poorest man, and he sees that he is not alone. I was taken aback once more how a man with nothing had such a deep acceptance of this world that has so much. Here was someone who had emerged from the vicious caste system only to then fight for his children to do the same. And yet he accepted his limitations, even as he struggled against them.

"Because," he explained, "if I am good and honest person, God might send help for me."

We all know what's next, right? I thanked Dilip for his help, for his kindness, and most of all for showing me how to live in acceptance of the moment that I am in. Maybe acceptance and struggle didn't have to be in conflict. Maybe I could, in the same breath, accept my home, and yet be willing to question it. Be willing to always question my own comfort, my own happiness. It was in that questioning, that I might not feel complacent.

I explained to Dilip about the other part of my trip, the part about giving back.

I took in a deep breath before I continued, "You see, to me, education isn't just about learning things in school. It is about learning about life. It is about learning to reach beyond what our parents have and, and . . . it's about learning how to dream. So what I would like to do, if you agree, is to pay for the education of both your sons until they are eighteen years old."

Dilip's smile disappeared. "Eighteen years old?" he mumbled.

At first, I worried he might be upset, so I tried to explain it a different way, "Yes, I will pay for the education of both your sons for the next fifteen years."

"It's hard to take in," Dilip began to rock back and forth slowly staring out at the water.

Suddenly, I found myself trying to convince him, as though he might not understand why I offered the gift, "You told me that you don't want your children to do what you do. You told me that you were kind because you never knew what would happen if you were kind to someone. You say you pray every day to God to change your life. So now your children will have the opportunity to live an educated life."

I kept talking until I saw a slow smile begin to wash over his face, tears circling his eyes as he nodded his head, taking it all in. He looked me deep in the eyes, and he began to laugh, "You help my children? You take care of my sons' future and their education? I'm very happy! I feel very happy. I tell my wife, she'll be so happy . . . so happy."

His excitement was contagious. He knew even more than I did what that gift could offer, because it wasn't just about giving a gift to one person. Like the energy of the village, the gifts were music that many might share. Just as Dilip had broken the mold and became a riverboat driver, so his sons would break the mold and go to school. Who knew how many times that torch would light another torch? How one decision might affect the next? All I could hope for, as I saw the love in Dilip's eyes that he had for his children, was that I had offered a little spark for their fire.

I hugged Dilip and his two sons, and asked Amrit to send me a card every year telling me how school is going. And that's how I ended up giving the one thing I always hated and for which I am begrudgingly grateful: school.

CHAPTER NINE

"Man is fond of counting his troubles, but he does not count his joys. If he counted them up as he ought to, he would see that every lot has enough happiness provided for it."
— Fyodor Dostoevsky

"Watch out," the Englishman warned. "I was robbed in Patna."

Benji leaned casually against the gas station wall, his arms burned from days walking in the scorching sun. He was on his own life-affirming trek, walking across the whole of India.

I will repeat.

Walking. Across. The. Whole. Of. India. Either this chap was a total madman or a complete genius. I must say, I never really figured out which one.

Benji had just bought me gas thirty miles outside the city of Patna, in the Bihar province — my next destination and the site of his robbery.

He looked around the barren station, where a bored attendant sat at a window selling empty plastic bottles filled with gasoline and occasionally with water. After his happy little tale of getting robbed in the town I was heading to, he reminded me why theft in India wasn't something to be angry over: "Always remember that there is someone out there less fortunate than you. Less healthy than you. Less lucky than you."

Benji slipped his sunglasses back on and adjusted his heavy backpack. I thanked him for the gas and wished that we were both heading in the same direction, but he was heading north as I continued east, east across the world.

I started up Kindness One and tried to ignore his earlier comment: "I got robbed in Patna." Of course, outside of Kindness One and my computer, I didn't have much to steal. Then again, that was pretty much everything.

Benji had also told me that Bihar province was one of the most dangerous places in India. So far, I had been warned of many impending dooms without actually running into one. The world is always more foreboding from a distance, but I also knew that time and place had as much to do with my safety as anything else. Tragically, five days after I left Patna, a bomb exploded killing five people.

India will always feel flat in words, because it isn't contained by language. It is written in color. It is drawn by sound. India breaks through all of the senses because India is filled with people. So many people.

I arrived in Patna in the middle of a religious festival, which meant people were swarming its streets, dashing and cheering between honking cars. Beet-red saris and bright-green silk clapped through the air like thunder as an assemblage of heavily armed Indian soldiers ("for protection of people," I was told) played bass to the dancers' treble.

For a moment I had to pinch myself to make sure I wasn't, in fact, in the middle of a Bollywood set, and not the town I had been so clearly forewarned about.

Kindness One and I were swept up in the sea of people until we were spit out onto a quieter street, where I tried to find some help — *tried* being the key term. I think one man's response summed it up best: "You're coming from America and say you have no money! How can that be possible? You're asking for food and all these things. There is much money you should have!"

The hard part was I *did* have money. Just not money *on me.* I had to keep reminding myself that I was giving back on this journey, otherwise my conscience would have got the better of me. I had long learned that sometimes having a dream means you have to be selfish — you have to do things that aren't always going to fit your ideals or your conscience or what other people think should be the vision of your life. Having a dream means taking a risk; it means going to dangerous places — whether that be a city called Patna or places within our own hearts. Coming to India with no money wasn't an easy task. In fact, it was a heartbreaking one. But I also knew it was the only way for me to the meet the rickshaw driver or the riverboat captain. It was the only way for me to meet India.

I walked back through the festival as the music moved through me, calming my anxiety and igniting my hope that help might still be on its way.

Then it happened. Again. My bike stopped working on a crowded street. You might be getting used to this, but I wasn't.

Anyway, you probably think you know what's coming. Screaming Indians. Lots of honking. But as I pulled my hulking yellow beast through the mass of sweaty bodies and scooters and, yes, more cows, starting my walk of shame to yet another mechanic's shop, I noticed that no one was yelling at me. Nobody. In fact, they were smiling, many of them standing back to let me pass. If only my Greek friends had been so kind. I finally stopped to ask someone, "Why are they are not screaming at me? I am used to being screamed at!"

"The yellow bike they like," an Indian traveler bellowed at me from his rickety old Vespa. "It's famous celebrity in India!"

For a moment, I thought Kindness One's reputation had begun to precede it, but the man continued, "Famous Bollywood movie film made on yellow bike."

It turned out that my bike really was famous. A similar yellow bike (probably a distant cousin of Kindness One) had appeared in a movie, and the revelers of Patna had apparently all seen it, leaving them in a trance as I dragged my defeated motorbike through its crowded streets.

People patted Kindness One as I walked through the throngs, wobbling their heads and touching me in awe. I was so surprised by the attention that I almost forgot Kindness One's current condition. A condition that I feared might be terminal.

All of a sudden, I felt a sense of hope that maybe all this love for Kindness One would give it the energy to start again. I pulled over and got on the bike, ready to hear its little engine roar. Instead what I heard was the dead-end click that had started this latest long and weary chapter. A man saw me struggling and asked in English if I needed a mechanic. *Do I need a mechanic? I always need a bloody mechanic!*

After another long day of rejection, this stout man was the angel I had been waiting for. Together we pushed Kindness One two miles to a motorbike repair shop — a shop filled with vintage Royal Enfields. Royal Enfield is a famous English motorcycle that is now a mainstay of India. Like the English cab in Colorado, a little piece of my homeland was calling to me, gently saying, "You are in the right place."

I walked up to the mechanic and decided to manifest my own success, informing him, "You saved me. Thank you."

He looked confused, which was actually a good sign because it meant he understood me.

I explained my troubles in English, giving the mechanic and the three assistants that surrounded him the whole story — Los Angeles, New York, Atlantic Ocean, Turkey, cargo plane, India, broken-down bike.

The mechanic acted as though he heard this tale every day. Turning to the bike, he asked, "So it just won't start?"

I sighed, "It just won't start."

The mechanic was right. The whole of my trip mattered little next to that truth.

He walked around the bike again before announcing, "We'll have to check it. There are many causes, and it's not just the spark plugs that we check when the bike is not starting. It could be a lot of things."

It could be a lot of things — not the response I was looking for, yet I maintained hope, as only a fool would do, "So can you fix my bike?"

At this point, more young men had joined the head mechanic. I couldn't tell if they also worked in the shop or were just intrigued by the pseudo-Bollywood star sitting in the middle of the garage, but the group of them began to wobble their heads in affirmation. I looked to the head mechanic to see if he agreed with his newly arrived sidekicks. He looked up and cocked his head to the right, "Yes."

"But there's one thing I need to tell you . . ." I began.

After the group heard that I had no money, they all convened to discuss the

221

matter in Hindi. From time to time, one of them would point in my direction — some eyed me like I was a lamb off to the slaughterhouse. Others gestured toward me with more compassion. My fate was in the balance until the head mechanic uttered the two most beautiful sentences on earth: "We can fix it with no money. You are driving famous bike machine."

All right, confession time. There was another reason why the mechanics thought I was famous. So far on the trip I had asked my camera crew to hang back, but on this one, I asked them to step forward. I wasn't just asking these mechanics for a bite to eat. I was asking them for a full-fledged motorbike overhaul. I didn't know what was wrong with the bike. All I knew was that it was something big that needed to be fixed. And something I was hoping would be fixed that day.

If that meant bringing out the camera crew, well, sometimes you just got to cheat. And sometimes cheating works. The magic of my little Bollywood star (and my production team) had charmed its way into the hearts of a small army of Indian mechanics.

Over the next eight hours, they took Kindness One apart. Literally, the bike was lying in pieces all over the dirt floor of the mechanic's shop. I went outside like a worried relative at the hospital. As I found out, the problem went much deeper than spark plugs (though they weren't in the best of shape, either). It went right into the filtration system, which, as one of the mechanic's assistants tried to explain, "was much hardness to fix." After running for so many days, I didn't know how to sit still. I spent most of those long hours pacing, hoping that Kindness One might make it out of this alive.

Finally, one of the mechanics came out and announced, "Sire, we must need presence of your good self."

I walked over and asked the head mechanic, "Have you fixed my baby?"

For the first time all day, he smiled at me with his tobacco-stained teeth. I wanted to kiss him after he replied, "Yes we have fixed it, good friend."

We wheeled the bike outside to where we held a ceremony to confirm that Kindness One would start. The bike roared back to life! The deafening applause of the crowd lifted my spirits and followed me as I rode back into the mayhem of Patna's festival. Though the sun was beginning to set, the crowds had yet to slow. I realized that in all my hours of waiting at the mechanic's, I had forgotten to secure a place to stay for the night. Motorbike hospitals can have that effect.

The sun was quickly disappearing, and I had few options as to where to rest for the night. It appeared I had used up all of Patna's generosity in getting my motorbike fixed, which was fine by me. I was still pinching myself that it was done at all.

As I drove, looking for one of the quieter streets I could find, I realized how much I had accomplished without any money, without any gas, without a cell phone. I remembered when I was first dating Lina, we were sitting at dinner together, and as was the norm for me back then, she was reading the menu while I was busy scrolling through my phone. Finally, I looked up to find her staring at me.

"You can have dinner with me," she said with a sly smile. "Or you can have dinner with your phone. It's your choice."

My phone had become my easy way out from paying attention to the world around me. I would fall down the rabbit hole of emails and text messages and status updates, and I would lose sight of the people right in front of me. I would fail to hear how their day had gone. I would miss the point when they told me about something they had read or something they had seen. I would ignore that they wanted the one thing from me that I continually spouted that I wanted from others: connection.

I didn't realize it at the time, but my phone, my computer, all that false connectivity was really just another mask, the way I separated myself from those around me, and here was this woman on one of our first dates saying to me, "Drop the mask."

I stopped on a quiet Indian road, Kindness One humming beneath me, and I realized that this is what happens when we drop the mask. We show our best selves, and we invite others to do the same. That day, I had not only seen the generosity of those mechanics and their care for my precious yellow bike, I had also been connected into that extraordinary web of kindness, one that I often failed to see at home, but had found here in India.

I thought back to Benji's warning from just that morning: "I got robbed in Patna." Well, now I was really going to test the city's kindness. I was going to be sleeping in a yellow motorbike on the side of one of its bustling roads — although sleeping would probably not be the correct word. As I tried to fall into a hazy slumber, I found myself awoken by many festival goers just walking home from the day's celebration. Some even took photos of the crazy Englishman sleeping in his yellow bike. I couldn't blame them. We had become quite famous.

If asked, most people probably couldn't find the country of Bhutan on the map. I couldn't even find the country of Bhutan on the map. But back when I was looking at the great map of the world that scrolled across the edges of my desk in LA, I noticed one interesting little blip just to the northeast of India, and that blip was Bhutan.

As I soon found out, Bhutan is not just a brief commercial break in the long TV program known as India. It is also home to the inspiring and equally humbling concept known as "Gross National Happiness." As soon as I heard the words, I felt like I was back on Hollywood Boulevard, staring at the homeless man's sign. Bhutan wasn't just a place I wanted to visit. It was a place that I wanted to make a part of me. It was a place I felt like I was already a part of.

In Bhutan, they determine the success of their country by the happiness of their people. It's not about wealth. Or power. Or their GDP. The concept of Gross National Happiness was built on the foundation of how love and kindness are traded between their people, and how that trade — not of money and goods, but of real human connection — brings the one thing you can't trade: joy.

But before I made it there, I would have to survive the remaining Indian roads and the many hundreds of miles that still stood between Bhutan and me. What would have been a twelve-hour journey in most other parts of the world, turned into a three-day trek involving stray cows, irate truck drivers, random potholes, and a fleet of wild geese!

Over the next three days, I saw the map that was once scrolled across my desk come to life. My first stop was in Darjeeling. I don't think the queen would have been very happy with me if I didn't pay a visit to the birthplace of Indian tea. I visited a tea farm, drank some delicious local tea, and found a nice Englishman to stay with. But more than that, I found a sense of calm that I had yet to discover in India. My trip seemed to slow down. After running from city to city, I felt my whole body begin to relax as I drove along the rural roads to Bhutan.

I could feel the stress of the previous few weeks dissipate. The stress of walking a broken-down motorbike through clogged streets, the worry over finding a place to sleep, the fear of being robbed or beaten or worse — all of it seemed to fade away into the deep quiet of the Indian countryside and the steep mountain passes rising up to greet me, gently reminding me of their strength.

My final night on the road before reaching Bhutan was spent in Kindness One, again. I had been riding for so many hours that I just veered off the Indian death trap — otherwise known to you and me as a road — and fell asleep. Apart from the trucks whizzing past me, it was quite a good night's rest — as good as can be expected when your life is in the hands of an army of sleep-deprived Indian truck drivers.

The day I had first found Bhutan on a map, I quickly dashed off an email to a friend, who, through another contact, connected me to one of the Bhutanese government ministers. They had graciously emailed the minister, explaining my trip and how I felt that Bhutan was my Shangri-la, how it spoke to the very nature of my journey. And how it showed that kindness wasn't just a gesture between people, but that it could also be the foundation for an entire country.

After a few weeks, I had nearly forgotten that the email had been sent when we received a response from someone at the Minister of Environment's office. Even he spoke the language of kindness, explaining in his email that the whole world lives in goodness; cruelty is the distraction. He told me that my story was at the heart of Bhutan's beliefs and that he couldn't wait to meet me to hear more about my journey.

Yes, sometimes the computer *can* connect people.

And six months later, there I was in Bhutan. The building where the minister worked was a simple bungalow at the foot of a very tall mountain. I could feel my heart begin to race as I walked into the windowless conference room where we would be meeting.

When the minister entered the room, I felt the weird yet comforting sense that I had been there before. In many ways, it was like what I had always wanted home to feel like: safe and loving with no judgment or fear. I had ached for this my whole life, and now as I sat across the table talking about a culture that believed in finding the joy in every moment, in creating kindness through connection, I knew that it wasn't home I had been running from; it was a different kind of home that I had been running to.

The minister spread out his hands as

though to show me the openness of his people, sharing about his country, "You can go to any house, anywhere; they will always welcome you. No matter how poor, they will take out their best for you. They will make you feel at home. They will offer you a bed; they will offer you food; they will offer you a drink. This is the true essence of Gross National Happiness."

I understood the concept. I had been experiencing it for months. Kindness and joy danced every day across the world, and as I had seen in Delhi, in Varanasi, in New York, it was often those who offered the most kindness who also seemed to experience the most happiness, despite the poverty or tragedy or desperation they might otherwise face.

The minister agreed. Touching his heart, he said, "Because it's coming from here. This is the value system. If we lose it, it's gone forever. No amount of money in the world can bring it back."

I had seen that, too — most particularly in myself. And maybe that is why even in the moments when I was most embarrassed to be traveling through such impoverished communities with no money in my pocket, I knew that I couldn't have done this trip any other way. As much as everyone in the world should have clean water to drink, and safe and stable roofs over their heads, and an education for their children, below that, deep in the cement of our foundation as human beings, is a happiness that cannot be bought.

As the minister clarified, Bhutan didn't celebrate Gross *Individual* Happiness; they celebrated Gross *National* Happiness.

He sat back in his chair and nodded in my direction as he explained, "But know it is not just here in Bhutan that kindness occurs. People are changing everywhere; society is changing, and so the focus changes."

"You're a very wise man," I replied, having seen those same changes in myself — not just in who I was, but also in how I viewed the world.

"No," the minister laughed. "I just pay attention."

But maybe wisdom really is just paying attention.

The small moments, the small acts, the small changes. We always think that change needs to come in broad strokes. That in order to follow your dreams, you need to get on a yellow motorbike to cross the world on kindness, but maybe the real epiphany is to pay attention to all the dreams unfolding around us. If I could make one promise to myself, I decided it would be this: when I got home, I would leave the bloody phone alone. I would pay attention. I would let my heart break open a little more. I would allow myself to be happy.

I left the building and drove through the winding mountains and draped greenery of the Bhutanese countryside. I could feel small drops of dew on my face, the wet breeze through my jacket, cooling my skin. I could hear the faint revving of trucks and cars moving behind me on the narrow pass. I decided I wanted to meet one of the citizens of Bhutan. I wanted to see Gross National Happiness in the flesh, and because I'm a bit of a cynic at times, I wanted to test the minister's assertion that, "You can go to any house, anywhere, they will always welcome you."

I pulled up to a small farmhouse and saw a man on a tractor. I quickly found out that he didn't speak great English (although it was probably better than my Bhutanese). He sent me to speak to his son, Bikash, who was in his early twenties and spoke enough English for us to communicate.

After I told Bikash about my quest, he immediately invited me inside for some tea, and as we sat in his warm living room next to a burning fire, while the weather outside grew darker with rain, I asked him about his own experience with Gross National Happiness.

Bikash smiled broadly, as though I had just brought up his favorite football team: "Different people have different opinions about Gross National Happiness. For me, it's being at home with my family, having three meals in a day. My family is happy. This means happiness to me."

"So happiness equals simplicity?" I asked.

"Yes, exactly," he replied.

"We should tell the rest of the world that."

"Yes, we should," Bikash laughed.

So I am telling you now. In fact, I am telling myself now, lest I forget again. Happiness equals simplicity. It's so easy to want to complicate life, to think that happiness is an impossibly long calculus equation that only the truly brilliant or truly successful or truly spiritual can solve, but I realized that if a half-educated chap like me could achieve it, maybe the formula wasn't so complicated, after all.

Bikash invited me to stay the night, offering me dinner as well. I couldn't help but laugh — if only all my travels had been so easy.

"Tell me," I asked. "Are all Bhutanese people this friendly and this happy?"

Bikash replied matter-of-factly, as though I had just asked him if the sun was yellow. "Yes, all are like me. They're jolly; they're friendly; they're good. That's why this is the Land of Happiness."

I had been traveling the world seeking and finding kindness. But now, I was in its mecca. In so many ways, I felt like this moment was the pinnacle of my journey. I had found within this little country a dream I didn't even know I had: to sit by a fire with a laughing stranger, sharing a cup of tea on a rainy afternoon in a place that felt like the best of home.

Leaving Bhutan, I knew that maybe it was time to create a new idea of home. Not one that fit so tightly I felt like I couldn't breathe. Maybe it was by reconnecting to this adventure, that I would always be on it. That night, I scrolled through my address book, through all the names and numbers and emails I had collected, knowing that no matter where I went in this world (including the fine city of Los Angeles), those memories, those connections would always be there.

The next morning, I breathed in the clean mountain air, bracing myself for my return to the busy and dirty streets of India. I had fallen in love not just with the external beauty of Bhutan, which was indeed magnificent, but also with the internal beauty of its people — with their faith, their joy, their deep connection not just to each other, but also to the knowledge that we are all only here for a brief and blistering moment. We come to dance and sing and see our hearts get broken over and over again. And then we leave this body behind, the light that lives within us either being extinguished into nothingness, or living on in some other form. Either way, we will never be here in the same time, or the same way, again.

"Goddamn it!" I yelled, nearly kicking Kindness One in the head, which, for once, wasn't actually to blame for my frustration. The culture shock of returning to India had hit me hard. Gone was the serenity of Bhutan — *adios* to happiness and joy.

Just in case you aren't up on your South Asian geography (as I certainly wasn't), Calcutta is a massive detour from Bhutan. But I was a man on a mission, and a man on a mission cannot be stopped — even by the perilous roads of India.

I had just been driven off the road by a goat herder and a motorbike filled with people. There must have been at least four adults and two children on that bike. Both Kindness One and I almost careened into a wall, stopping just before we took out the side of someone's home.

I had spent too many hours on Kindness One. My legs were numb. My jacket was drenched from the vestiges of a monsoon rainstorm. My head hurt. And there I was, freshly arrived in Calcutta, and people were already running me off the road.

After I stopped swearing and the small crowd that had gathered to watch me began to disperse, I remembered why I had come to Calcutta in the first place. If you might remember, I had a bit of a moment in Kosovo with a statue of Mother Teresa and had decided that I would make it to the city she had adopted as her home. I would go to the charity that she founded, and I would hopefully get out of these wet clothes.

I started up Kindness One and tried to maintain my calm as I worked my way across town to meet Mother Teresa. And that's exactly what I did. Or rather, I was able to visit her tomb. Walking around the mission she founded, I felt again that warmth I had met in Bhutan. I stood in the room where she had made so many changes in this world of ours, where she had experienced a vision of peace that few others had ever seen.

As I was walking out of the house, I stopped to read a letter Mother Theresa had written. In it, she said, "It's not how much we give but how much love we put into giving." I stepped back, feeling the weight of her words press down on me.

When I went back out on the crowded street, I was ready again to take on India. I decided to go for a walk and try to find something to nibble on. What I found instead was a man who operated an orphanage for children. Barik was turning a corner when he literally ran into me.

He wobbled his head and apologized, "So sorry, sir."

"Oh no," I responded. "That was my fault. I'm just a bit lost."

Barik stopped and asked, "How so?"

Well, my friend, let me tell you. It didn't take long for Barik's story to trump my own. He ran an orphanage for children whose parents had either died or abandoned them to the vagaries of life on the streets of India.

"So many children," he shrugged. "We try to help, you see."

I decided that I *would* see, and followed him back to the orphanage, where I was quickly greeted by dozens of smiling faces. I couldn't believe how many children there were. They all circled me, laughing and pointing, giggling and hiding as Barik introduced me to the few brave enough to meet this new stranger.

Barik was probably in his early thirties, but there was a light in his eyes that echoed the joy of the children around him. We started playing cricket in the yard, where Barik joined in, right alongside the kids.

"Who helps all these children?" I asked him, in awe of how many orphans lived in this run-down building in the center of town.

Barik stood back from the game as he answered the question, "Local people help. Many people give the children rice, meat, bread, money . . ."

"But what about you?" I asked. "Why did you decide to help the children?"

"I help with many things for them — driving them, teaching school."

Barik then changed the subject, clearly humbled by his own work. Instead, he asked if I needed a place to stay. "We have apartment for the teachers," he explained. "You can stay with us."

I thought again of Mother Teresa's quote as I watched Barik help the children put away their used and broken toys. He put so much love into his giving, offering a committed care to these children, who had little else. And I saw that despite what had happened to them, despite how they came here, the children offered the greatest gift in return: their laughter. As we ate our curry and rice dinner together, seated on the floor, as is Indian tradition, their joy was infectious. They had food before them and friendship around them. They had teachers who loved them — a family of strangers perhaps, but a family nonetheless. After dinner the children lined up to drink water from a fountain. I had learned to always ask in India about the water before drinking it, but this time I moved to get in line before Barik stopped me, "No, water not safe."

"For me?" I asked.

"Not safe for anyone."

"But the children are drinking it," I was confused as I watched a small boy lean forward to sip from the faucet.

"No safe. Children get sick too."

I found out that it was the only water they had. That even though the children regularly got sick from drinking it, they had no choice.

I went to sleep that night, hearing the children cough in the other room. At one

239

point, a young girl got up and vomited in a trashcan. It quickly erased the memory of their laughter just a few short hours before.

When I awoke, there was no hesitation in my mind. I was going to give back to this man and the children under his care. If ever one gift could affect so many, I knew that the future of these children might be altered by the smallest change in their current lives, just as Barik had already done.

Barik and I walked outside to the courtyard where the kids were having breakfast, and I thanked him for coming to my rescue, "The children have joy in their eyes, and you have given them hope, and that is a wonderful thing."

I realized that it was hope I saw in Barik's eyes; it was hope I saw in the eyes of the children. Maybe what we see as childlike innocence is really just that. It is the naiveté of hope. The pure and honest belief that life can and always will get better. As we get older, so many of us begin to doubt that hope. We prepare for the worst. We worry about losing our jobs, not making enough money. We worry about our mothers and children, and wives and husbands. For me, I worried a lot about Kindness One. And in that great swell of "what if," we forget about what *is*.

I explained to Barik that I wanted to offer them a gift. When he told the children, they quickly gathered around. It was my first gift to have an audience of so many and so young.

I had realized while playing with the children the day before that they needed more equipment, so I told him, "The first thing I want to do is I am going to buy lots of sports equipment: footballs, cricket bats, badminton rackets . . . lots of sport things."

Barik looked at me in disbelief and then translated the good news to the kids. A cry went up as the boys quickly began swinging imaginary bats at the thought of having real ones.

And then I explained the second gift: I wanted to buy them new purifiers for the water so that the children would no longer get sick.

Barik hugged me, and another big cheer came from the kids.

"There's one last thing," I said. "When you took me on the tour of the home, you told me about the school and you said to me that you didn't have many books. For me, books changed my life. As a kid, I used to read all the time. So what I have decided to do is to stock your library with one thousand new books."

By this time, the kids had surrounded us, jumping up and down and bellowing in excitement. Barik was left speechless. I understood. Because hope lives in us as long as we believe that life can — and will — get better. Even when it seems that our dreams are impossibly far off in the distance, and we don't know how we're going to get there, the right person, the right miracle will always appear if we wait for it. You never know: one day a bald man with an English accent might just show up on a yellow motorbike, or a quiet man named Barik will find you sleeping on the streets, and that hope — that bright little flicker of light in your eyes — will be restored.

CHAPTER TEN

"You can't run away from trouble. There
ain't no place that far."
— Uncle Remus

"Are you sure?" I stood in the front office
of the orphanage on the phone with Lina.
Only the day before, I had been denied a
visa for Burma. Before leaving LA, I had attempted to get every possible visa I would
need. The only problem was, I ran out of
time to get one for Burma. But when I
called the Burmese consulate in Washington,
DC, they had said not to worry, that I could
get the visa while in India. Apparently, they
were wrong, or rather, wrong-*ish*.

You see, *some* people in India could get
them. It just depended where you were and
what border you were attempting to cross.
It also depended on what time of day it was
and who was working that shift. In a country
with 1.2 billion people, several hundred

languages, and a distorted view of modern management, Indian logistics were famous for their entire lack of logic. And I was slap-bang in the middle of all the chaos.

Which is what led to me calling Lina in the middle of her night, hoping that she could secure something through the Burmese consulate in Washington. Unfortunately, her phone call hadn't gone so well.

"They said you would have to be here, in person," she paused before continuing. "Maybe if we were married, it would be different, but since we're not even related, they said there wasn't much they could do."

Ouch (good one, Lina). But as much as it hurt, I knew she was speaking the truth. As I neared the end of my journey, that fateful return home edging closer, I could also feel her beginning to wonder what she was waiting for. I mean, I understood her wanting to get married, and in this instance, it might have even allowed her to secure a Burmese visa (although doubtful) for me, but I also knew, well, quite simply, that I was afraid.

It wasn't that I didn't want to have children or a life partner. Lina and I had been together for a number of years, but we had just moved in with one another only months before this journey. And marriage sounded so . . . permanent.

Did settling down mean that I would be also, well, just, settling? Not for Lina — she was the love of my life — but rather for that cookie-cutter existence I had been trying to deny ever since my first dreams of escaping "real" life had emerged. I couldn't help but wonder if making the ultimate commitment might turn into that oak-filled London office? Would I find myself staring out the window of my relationship, wondering if I had exchanged my dreams just because I was following the path that everyone else expected me to? Even demanded.

"You can still do both," Lina had told me during one of our last conversations before I left LA, and as I sat on the other end of that line in the front office of an orphanage, I wondered again whether I could honestly keep this adventure going and still have my emergency contact back at home. Was that being true to myself or was that just being selfish?

"I'll figure something out," I replied confidently, but I knew Lina could hear the fear in my voice. What the hell was I going to figure out?

Since Calcutta was a port city, I thought of trying to bypass Burma by boat. I took out my laptop and fired off an email to my shipping company contacts. And then I went out for a long walk around Calcutta. I felt trapped. It felt like the frenzied streets were closing in on me. It reminded me of when I was a kid at school, the classroom too small, the other kids too loud, my heart beating too fast, and my legs just wanting to run home as fast as I could. But then home was no more comforting. I arrived there only wanting to run back to school — never happy except for that time in between.

I stopped walking. And it felt like the whole of Calcutta stopped with me. Mother Teresa once said, "Love begins by taking care of the closest ones — the ones at home." For so long, I had run from home thinking that my job in life was to be done somewhere else. That in the "somewhere else" I would be happy. Home was the unhappy place, and the open road was the happy one. But if I looked back at the last few months, my greatest joys hadn't come from asking people for help, or from that great unending road. No, they had come when I was connecting with others. When I found communion. When I discovered a place within me that was safe and gentle and filled with hope — that soft, quiet space called "home."

And suddenly, it was as if all the gifts materialized before me. I realized they weren't just about helping people to fulfill their dreams. In most of the cases, they were about helping people reconnect to their homes. Whether it was giving a home to Tony in Pittsburgh, or helping Bekim save his farm in Montenegro, or offering Dheeru a better home in Delhi, the gifts were just as much about where we come from as where we're going.

Maybe it was time for me to start connecting in a new way to mine. Maybe that was the difference between feeling trapped and getting to have my cake and eat it too. Because why on earth would I buy a cake if I wasn't planning to eat it? Though it was so easy for me to connect with someone I barely knew, it was time I started connecting with the people I loved. As the final legs of my journey began to appear before me, I knew that, as much as I wanted that freedom to run, the freedom to follow my dreams, I also wanted to know that someone had my back while doing it. But more importantly, I also wanted them to know that I had theirs.

I got back to the orphanage and checked my emails. One of my amazing shipping contacts had come through — the company would be able to provide me space on a ship heading to Thailand in three days. I had three days in Calcutta, and then I would be on my way east. I felt like I was in a Jason Bourne movie. As I soon found out, getting from Burma into Thailand might have been impossible anyway. Something to do with a drug war and a closed border. Although overcoming these obstacles might have been a small feat for Bourne, Logothetis was a bit more cautious.

To a certain extent, we all dream of paradise — that place of small-moving kindnesses, with white sandy beaches and the warm waters lapping against our knees. Before even arriving in Thailand, I had it pictured in perfect detail. I thought that, between the tourists visiting from across the world and the plethora of hotels that might be interested in hosting a man on a mission, paradise would soon be mine.

Paradise was not mine. In fact, paradise was a brutal wake-up call. I rode to the seaside resort of Pattaya to try my luck, only to discover two things. One, most Thais do not speak English, which makes sense since they live in Thailand. Second, being a tourist without money created great cause for suspicion.

I went into a Western-looking hotel to ask for help, and before I knew it, the receptionist was picking up the phone to call the police. I wasn't sure if she was concerned that I had run out of money or that I was simply deranged, but either way, I decided it was better not to tangle with the local authorities in order to find out.

Like in India, the locals were confused by a Westerner with no money. I realized that in paradise, most tourists come to spend cash on food and hotels, not ask for free meals and a night's stay. I decided to change my target population, and began to ask foreigners, or *falung* as they are called in Thailand, for help. Finally, a friendly German stopped long enough to listen to me.

"No problem," he replied. "I'll take my daughter to school, and then I get you."

Sounded great to me, but as the minutes clicked by and Cornelius failed to return, I realized that my new friend had decided against helping his fellow European comrade.

Prior to arriving in Thailand, really the only major knowledge I had of it was drawn from the Leonardo DiCaprio movie *The Beach*. Not a real reliable source, I know. But still, I remembered that endless cerulean water, the hint that heaven could exist on earth, and if you've ever seen the movie, the reality that really scary shit can happen in foreign lands, especially in dingy hostel rooms! I decided to leave that part out of my fantasy of Thailand, and had headed to the beach instead.

I waded out in the warm water and looked back at the lush landscape that surrounded me. If ever there was a place to be without accommodation, this was it. The sun was receding into the sea behind me, and only a few other tourists swam in the clear water. I remembered the last line of the film, where Leonardo's character talks about finding paradise, "And me? I still believe in paradise. Because it's not where you go. It's how you feel for a moment in your life when you're a part of something. And if you find that moment . . . It lasts forever."

I had made it 16,955 miles (approximately) around the world. I had no place to stay. I had no money. I had no one to talk to, but I couldn't have been happier. It was like the old man had said in Varanasi, "Live inside this moment, and do not lose this time." I was inscribing it forever within me, memorizing the temperature of the water, the feel of the breeze across my face, the sound of the birds flying high above. I was alive and present and whole. I felt like Odysseus again, moving between exotic locales, knowing that home was getting closer, and like Odysseus, though a part of me wanted to return there, I also wondered if I could ever give this up.

As I got out of the sea I watched the final embers of the sun disappear into the vastness of blue, and decided that I would sleep on the beach. The weather was warm and the people friendly, so why not? It wasn't the best night's sleep, but it was certainly not the worst. You remember Patna, don't you?

When the morning sun lifted itself above the green canopies of Pattaya, I decided to head toward the capital of Bangkok. If I thought India was a culture shock, Bangkok was like walking out of a monastery and into a Rolling Stones concert. Scooters flew by me; drivers honked for no apparent reason; crowded buses teamed everywhere; rickshaws shared the road with a fleet of modern cars: Hondas and Mercedes and BMWs honking and pushing their way through a cacophony of traffic. It was at once a thoroughly modern city and also one filled with people still pushing carts of vegetables.

I headed off to backpack row: Khao San Road, where I quickly found someone to put me up for the night and went out to see the nightlife so vaunted by travelers the world over. As you might remember, *The Beach* also made Bangkok famous for less idyllic reasons. I was too tired to have that much fun in Bangkok. I returned back to the cheap hostel room someone had kindly rented for me to get some sleep before another day of travel.

In the morning I headed toward the old city of Ayutthaya, the former capital of Thailand. The pyramid-like temples stood from an altogether different time, reaching up to the sky like giants in prayer. The old stone pyres were intricately designed with the faces of Buddhist figures, reminiscent of the statues and gargoyles of Notre Dame. There I met a local man, Kamol, who ran a taxi service. He offered to take me to his village for lunch. I followed him a short way before we arrived in a small but thriving village that survived off an equally small but steady tourist industry.

Kamol and I took a walk around his village as he explained his plans to open up a restaurant in the nearby tourist town. Shots burst in the distance, making me instantaneously duck down.

"My wife, she makes very good Tom Kar Khai," Kamol explained, seemingly unfazed by the deafening sound.

I looked around, wondering why he hadn't

heard the large explosion that I had just heard. I asked him, "Is it safe here?"

"Oh, yes," he replied, rather confused, and then continued on. "We think maybe more *falung* would like good food."

More pops went off in quick succession, but Kamol didn't even flinch. I, on the other hand, was seriously frightened. I stopped walking, searching for a place to hide. Where were the shots coming from? I asked again, "Are you *sure* it's safe here? There's, like, gunshots."

More pops. At that point, I asked wide-eyed, "Can we go inside?"

Finally, Kamol realized what all the fuss was about. He started to laugh, "Fireworks! You scared of fireworks?"

I tried to regain my composure. No, I wasn't afraid of fireworks, but as you might remember, I knew bad things could happen even in paradise. Okay, yes, I was scared of fireworks!

Maybe because he was worried that, with my nerves, I might not make it through the night alone, Kamol offered me a place to stay. That night, I sat outside, alone in the darkened village. I could hear the clacking of pans as people cleaned up after dinner, children's voices echoing throughout the village. They were the sounds of everyday life. The kind that frankly terrified me, but suddenly, in this strange and beautiful place, it brought me comfort.

As I drove the next morning through the countryside to the Cambodian border, I couldn't help but remember my first days on Kindness One. As you might recall, I had lost my side mirror on one of those first days, which by the way, was still securely sleeping in my backpack. At the time, I wondered whether I would even make it out of New York. And here I was, driving through the rice fields of Thailand on my way to Cambodia. As much as the trip had been filled with these amazing experiences, I was still awed by them. I still am. As I made my way through Thailand, I was pulled over by a policeman — not for speeding, but simply because my bike was yellow.

"Yellow motorcycle is cool!" were his only words. I sometimes wondered how much love I would have received along my journey had my bike not been yellow. But then again, I did decide to buy a yellow bike in order to get as much attention as possible. Clearly, my plan had worked.

As I approached the border town, more and more people began driving alongside me. It was mayhem. But I like mayhem.

I pushed my bike up to the main gates,

gave my papers to the guards, and quickly realized that this was about to become a lot harder than I had expected.

You see, I wasn't the only one with a passport. Kindness One also had a passport, otherwise known as a *carnet.* And in order to cross a border with the bike, Kindness One's passport also needed to be stamped. And signed. And redelivered in one piece. So far I had had limited trouble with border crossings. Yes, I had had to pretend I supported my team's archenemies, Manchester United, to get past a drunken Albanian guard, but other than that, things had gone well. Until now, because my luck was about to change.

The first guard looked at Kindness One's carnet and then back at the bike. Something about one of the two did not make him happy. Also to top it off, the guard didn't speak much English. Or *any* English, for that matter. I tried to explain to him that in every country I had ridden through, people had signed for me, but it didn't seem to phase him. Of course it didn't. He had no idea what I was saying. But help was on the way. Or so I thought. My non-English-speaking border guard had gone to get reinforcements: eight other border guards. I hoped that at least one of them spoke

English. The new contingent of border guards huddled around my little piece of paper, talking quickly in Thai.

This back and forth went on for over an hour, as the sun faded into a dark and humid night. Things were not looking too good, and then, just before the office was about to close, the headman just took out a pen and signed. And then stamped. I was free.

"Really?" I exclaimed.

"Yes. You leave," the officer commanded.

I pushed the bike to the gates that would let me into Cambodia. Just one more person to charm, and I was on my way. Or so I thought. I would soon find out that *I thought wrong. Again.*

I handed over my freshly signed document to the final Thai border guard. The woman looked at the carnet and again looked at the bike and handed the carnet back to me, shaking her head, "No come through."

No come through? *I thought I just came through!*

It was about fifteen minutes before the border would close and I would be stuck in basically a no-man's-land between Thailand and Cambodia.

"But I already got this signed? The man next door, he —"

She cut me off swiftly, "Sorry. You no come through."

I had to think quickly. I decided to go back to the chief and beg him to come out and tell this lady that I was free to go and that my carnet had, in fact, been signed.

"Sorry," he said, echoing his comrade. "This not my job."

"Please, sir, you don't understand," I begged.

"No, you no understand. I go home now. My wife, she wait. Not my job."

Going home! This called for drastic action. I had to go rogue. And rogue I went. I hit my knees and clasped my hands together.

"No, sir, I have to get to Cambodia. Tonight. I have to get home. Please save me."

The man was putting papers into a bag, trying with all his might to completely ignore me. I knew if there was one thing people responded to it was this: children.

"My son," I lied. "I need to get home to my son!"

Look, I know it wasn't pretty, but it wasn't entirely untrue. Winston, my dog, was like a son to me, and I knew that he would be supremely upset if I never made it back home. But even my new son back home wouldn't change the guard's mind.

So I pretended to cry. Yes, I know — intensely desperate — but a man has to do what a man has to do! How else was I going to get through Cambodia and on my way back to America? I guess a strange English tourist with a yellow bike crying in the middle of your border station is bad for business because, before I knew it, the man finally sighed and said, "Okay, okay. Stand, please. I go talk."

I watched as the border guard walked the mammoth fifty feet to the other station, spoke quickly with the female guard, and then watched as she signed the carnet. Again. He even walked me to the gates, but I think that was just to be sure that the sobbing man who had already made him late to see his wife was actually gone for good. His parting words: "You leave." Fine with me.

I had made it into Cambodia. I was saved. Or should I say, once again, *I thought* I was saved. You see, the moment the Cambodian customs officials saw my yellow bike, they looked me up and down and sent Kindness One and me to the head of customs, just outside the border zone.

After pleading with another chap, pulling out the tears, and even adding an extra son to the tale, my yellow bike was still denied entry into Cambodia. It was 11:30 p.m., and they told me they had to go home but we could reconvene the negotiations tomorrow. I had two choices. Sleep in Kindness One or make a run for it.

And by "making a run for it," I mean that I was already officially in Cambodia, so all I had to do was drive Kindness One off into the countryside. I seriously contemplated this plan of action, but my senses got the better of me. I didn't want the Cambodian army coming after me, tanks and all, and how was Kindness One going to *get out* of the country without a signed document stating that she *got in*? Ending up in a Cambodian jail wasn't something I wanted to have on my résumé. So I decided to sleep it off and try again in the morning.

When morning came, I went back to the chief's office and tried again. I thought about giving him a brown envelope, but my brown envelope would have been just that, an empty brown envelope. Nothing more. Nothing less. In the end he let us both through. To this day I still have no idea why he changed his mind. Maybe he spoke to his wife and felt pity for my two sons waiting for me back home. Or maybe it was just fate.

I started my Cambodian adventure in earnest by driving to the legendary Angkor Wat. Built in the twelfth century, the cone-shaped temples were once the capital of the Khmer Empire, serving first as a Hindu place of worship and ultimately becoming a Buddhist temple. I met a kind German couple who paid my entry, and I found myself in the nine-hundred-year-old ruins, awed by man's ability to build something as magnificent as nature.

I walked through the stone pillars and felt that sense of calm that I had found in the seas off Pattaya. What a perilous few days I had had, adrenaline and fear pumping through my system, and now here I was on the other side of it. The sun began to set, and once again, I was reminded of just how small I was in the vastness of this world — its histories and mysteries. The overwhelming sculptures around me spoke to a greater permanence. These passing memories would die with me. Of course, that didn't mean I wouldn't try to share them. Maybe that's why I had to film everything, record every moment. I needed a witness for this life, for all the lives I was getting to be a part of.

I walked out onto the grounds in front of the temple and met a group of American missionaries who were on their own travels around the world. I soon found out that they were doing something called the "World Race."

One of the youths, a heavy-bearded chap in his early twenties explained, "You go to eleven countries, a month in each country. Last month we were in Thailand, the month before that we were in China, so this is our third month."

"That's amazing," I replied. "What have you learned on your travels?"

Each person in the group offered different answers — for the bearded fellow, it had only deepened his love for home, where freedom and convenience were paramount. Another offered, "I've learned a lot about love. And I guess I've learned, even in a short amount of time, that it doesn't matter where you come from or what your background is, you can still have joy."

I nodded. I had seen the same thing. I remember Dilip carrying his son in his arms, proud of the boy, the joy that his family brought, even though they still struggled to put food on their plates. I agreed with the young man, adding, "The sad part is, at home, we have so much materialism and yet often we have so little joy."

Maybe if nothing else, that was what I had learned in my travels across Southeast Asia.

Gross National Happiness was at the heart of that concept. In the United States (and, trust me, in England, too), it seems all we do is worry about what we don't have. *Buying* is how we prove to the world that we're okay. That we're happy. And yet, we are often disconnected. Removed from our innate desire for human contact. In many ways the web of kindness that is woven by those less fortunate becomes a much richer tapestry than the materialism we worship in more prosperous societies.

The group invited me to walk with them and later offered me a place to stay for the night. That night as we shared a meal (or rather they shared their meal with me), one of the young women said: "You know, the thing is, we're supposed to be here to help, but the people we've met, they've ended up giving more to us than we could ever have given to them."

How right she was.

I left my missionary friends the next day and continued on through Cambodia. Some days it felt as though I could ride Kindness One forever. And other days, I felt like I never wanted to look at that bloody bike again. That day in Cambodia was filled with more of the latter, as I begrudgingly bore toward the flat, unending horizon, hoping against hope that I might just find a place to sleep.

Finally, I pulled over at a gas station, where I met a local woman who bought me some much needed gas. Sophia offered to bring me to a village not far from where we were, but certainly off the beaten track. She said there was no doubt I could find a place to stay there, so I offered her a ride in my sidecar, and off we headed into the unknown.

As I had learned so many times on this journey, it was the spontaneous leaps of faith that often led to my deepest lessons. Though the village could hardly be found on a map, as people came out to greet me and offer me lunch, it seemed as though everyone in the village had roofs over their heads and food on their plates. All except one house.

Sophia pointed it out to me and explained who lived inside.

"Seng," she explained, "is a woman with only one child. Her husband die from AIDS, and now she has it."

Sophia took me to meet Seng. "How does she support herself?" I asked.

"She cannot do anything because of her illness," Sophia said

"What about her son?" I asked, wondering if he was also sick.

Sophia replied with the one dose of good news: "Her son not have HIV."

We entered Seng's small shack. The sides were made of tin, and the roof was made of loose boards. As we sat down to talk, with Sophia working as translator, I asked Seng how she was able to get food.

Sophia spoke briefly with Seng before reporting back: "Her relations give her food."

"And she lives in this house?" I asked, looking around at the open cracks in the roof and the fragile fabric of its walls. I couldn't help but add, "What happens when it rains?"

Seng motioned to the walls and imitated the rainfall coming through. The sadness in her eyes needed no translation.

I found out that Seng had no food to eat that night — that she and her son, Mai, only had enough food to eat lunch. They lived on the kindness of others — isolated by a disease that Seng had not even known existed until she contracted it. She gently stroked her son's hair — her last remaining connection to love.

"What do you want to see for the future of your son?" I asked through Sophia.

Sophia translated Seng's reply: "She wants

her son to study, but it is difficult because there's no money to support him to study."

When the rains came, they both got wet. When the winds came, their roof fell apart. Now, I knew why I had come to this village, because it had led me to this woman and the sad and lonely life she had been forced to live. Seng had already agreed that I could stay the night in their hut, sleeping on the raised bamboo platform. Sophia would stay nearby. There was little more to say. Words could never heal Seng's life, but I hoped to offer her something that might help.

I asked if Sophia would translate for me again as I explained to Seng how I tried to give back along my trip.

Sophia looked at me, waiting for me to speak. I wasn't sure how to say it, I wasn't even sure how I would pull it off, but I knew if I could only give one gift this entire trip, I would want it to be this: "I want to build Seng and Mai a new house."

Sophia explained to her what I had said, but both women seemed confused.

I explained further, "I will build her a proper house with tile floors and a place to cook and everything. She's never going to have to worry about her son sleeping in the rain again."

Sophia translated, shrugging her shoulders

as though her English were failing her.

"Does she understand?" I asked.

"Yes," Sophia said. "But you build house yourself?"

Apparently, they weren't too convinced of my construction abilities. Smart ladies. I told Sophia that I would make sure someone local did it. I wasn't quite the right chap for that particular job.

Again, Sophia translated, but this time, Seng wasn't confused by the words; she was confused by the gesture.

Sophia smiled, "She does not believe that someone would do this for her."

"You deserve this, Seng. You and Mai. You deserve a safe home."

As Sophia translated these last words, Seng's eyes filled with tears. Mai looked back and forth between Sophia and his mother, as though he, too, were just beginning to understand. Seng said something to Sophia in Khmer, the Cambodian national language.

Sophia smiled and explained, "She says thank you and that she will never forget you in her life."

Seng took hold of my hand, the tears now flowing down her face. We didn't need words. This was the type of moment that I had always been seeking. It wasn't out on the road with unending freedom. It was here, in Seng's hut. It was getting to pay attention to someone closely enough, that I not only learned about her life, I was able to become a part of it.

Mai came up to me and gave me a hug as he thanked me in both Khmer and English. Seng also began to smile through her tears, speaking again to Sophia.

Now it was Sophia's turn to start crying, "She said she's never lived in a proper house."

The missionary's words were wafting through my soul — I would learn so much more from the people I met than I could ever hope to teach them. The only thing I could do was humbly offer gratitude for the lesson.

Before leaving the next day, I gave Mai a ride in Kindness One. As the wind whizzed through his hair, I looked over to see him smiling. It was the first time I had seen him smile, and it was the memory of that joy that followed me down the dusty road as I restarted my journey to the capital of Cambodia, Phnom Penh. Meeting Seng had shown me just how isolated one human could be. I hoped that in offering her a home, she would feel connected again to life.

■ ■ ■ ■

I find that sometimes it takes a third party to restore us to our best selves. Sometimes we just can't do it ourselves, however hard we may try. I thought back to when I moved to Los Angeles to pursue my big dreams. Like for so many people who try to break the mold of their previous existence, things weren't going particularly well. I had come up with a big dream, which unfortunately had turned into big expectations. Big disappointment naturally followed. Those walls felt like they were closing in on me, so I decided I would find a new dream, out there, away from home.

Had I been with Lina at the time, I am sure she would have called it running. But I called it adventure. I was going to drive from London to Mongolia. The only snafu was that I had a near head-on collision with a Romanian driver. Death missed its intended target by inches. I lived. I returned to LA, nursing big physical wounds, but on top of that, some painful emotional ones too. I felt like I had failed.

Giving up seemed the best option. And it was tempting. So very tempting. All I had to do was pack my bags and head back to the desk job. It was safe, secure, and surrounded by familial love. I was single. And outside of my dog Winston, who could come back with me to London, I had no deep ties to my adopted home. I started making arrangements for our return and decided to have one last big party to say farewell to all my friends. Los Angeles had defeated me.

And then that night, as the party was drawing to a close, my life changed. In walked a blonde with messy hair. I don't know if you could call it love at first sight, but like that moment on the Calcutta Street, time seemed to stop. Over the next few hours, I told this woman about my trips around the world. I told her about my dreams. What I didn't tell her was that I was planning on leaving.

She looked me in the eyes and said, "I wish more people were like you. They seem to follow other people's dreams and give up on themselves way too easily."

If you haven't guessed it by now, that woman was Lina. And because of her, I ended up not giving up on my dream. For two reasons: First, because Lina doesn't like rain, and it rains in London far more than it doesn't; and second, because I had found someone who believed in me.

CHAPTER ELEVEN

"Man's goodness is a flame that can be
hidden but never extinguished."
— Nelson Mandela

My ride to the capital was uneventful. Although at this point, uneventful to me was probably a bit out of touch with reality. I spent the night with a Polish man who had moved to Cambodia after a messy divorce. He fed me, entertained me with stories about Polish heroism during World War II, and then sent me packing. You know — all in a day's work. The next afternoon, I arrived in Phnom Penh.

I had been to enough Asian cities by that point to expect the crush of humanity. The thick smell of frying foods and car exhaust. The honking of horns and the ever-climbing song of people yelling across food stalls and alleyways. But what I didn't expect was the enduring charm that lived in all the busyness of Phnom Penh. Because mixed in with the new and old Asia was also, surprisingly, an unmistaken flourish of old Europe, leftovers from Cambodia's harsh past under French rule.

But underneath the charm of a beautiful city and the friendliness of a beautiful people was a much darker story. As a kid I had grown up with stories of the Khmer Rouge and the atrocities committed in their name. During the Communist reign of Pol Pot in the mid to late 1970s, nearly two million people were executed out of a population of eight million. Persons from foreign countries, those with ties to foreign countries, to another political party, to intellectuals, artists, and anyone else who may or may not have been dissenters were sent to what were later named the "Killing Fields," holes in the ground that would be filled with as many as twenty thousand bodies at a time.

Though so much of my trip had been about kindness, about connecting, about coming together despite our differences, I knew that I couldn't pass through this part of the world and also not honor what happens in the void of all that goodwill. I had to go and see the consequences of believing that some lives should be valued more than others. That some lives don't mean anything at all.

When I arrived at the former killing field, I joined up with a tour group as they walked around. The guide told us about the horrors that took place in the absence of humanity. He described how the Khmer Rouge had brought prisoners out from the camp in green trucks, naked, with their eyes blindfolded and hands cuffed. When they stopped the trucks' engines they marched all of them to the exact spot where I was standing. The victims were forced to kneel at the edge of the pits, often already filled with the stench of rotting corpses. And then the orgy of killing would begin.

Innocent women, children, and men had been slaughtered on this very spot — by machetes, shovels, bamboo sticks, knives, and pickaxes. The Khmer Rouge tried never to use bullets. They believed that bullets were more precious than the lives they were taking away.

The tour guide continued with his gruesome story: "Around this pit, there was one terrible tree. It was 'The Killing Tree.' It was that tree there."

He pointed only a few feet from where we all stood, a group of English-speaking tourists of many nationalities — from Germany and Australia, India and America.

"The Khmer Rouge created a very traumatic killing here," he explained, his eyes dark as he told us the story. "They began to find things to entertain themselves. They know the mother's heart. It's always love for their baby. So those poor mothers were brought here together with the baby and children."

We all braced ourselves for what was surely to come. I wasn't sure I could stand to hear it. Again, that eternal optimist in me always wanted to believe that life could be a gentler place. How on earth do we reconcile its cruelties?

The tour guide told us what we already suspected, but feared to imagine: "The soldiers, they decided to remove the blindfold from the mothers' eyes, and they forced the mothers to open their eyes and watch the killing of their baby. They grabbed the baby's ankle like a chicken or frog and the killer just smashed the baby's head against the tree. They threw them up high into the air and they used the rifle's bayonet and they stabbed them."

He stopped for a moment. I imagined he had to tell this story frequently, a constant reminder of what had happened to his people — *by* his own people. It was as though he woke up every day in the same nightmare, haunted by the millions who had fallen into those shallow graves.

"But right here," he finally spoke. "We cannot even cry. The tears become blood because the mothers already watched the baby die."

We continued on the tour, and afterward I asked the tour guide how he managed to do this every day. How he lived telling this tragic story over and over.

"This is the story of my people."

"But doesn't it make you sad?" I asked. "It's the twenty-first century. We have the Internet, McDonald's, and here we are standing in front of bones that used to cover the entire field because someone decided to commit mass genocide. How do you go back to modern life after living in this past every day?"

"This is modern life, too," he reminded. "Maybe not here. Maybe no more. But somewhere, this is modern life."

He was right. Every day these atrocities continue to happen across the world. The wrong person comes to power. The people are poor and hungry and tired. And then they become convinced that things might be better if only the enemy among them were destroyed. And so good men do terrible things, thinking all along that what they are doing is right. And years later, tourists arrive and say the words that we have all said too many times: *never again.*

Our guide looked out to where we had just walked, passing the open ditches that once contained people he knew, people he might have loved. "I think it is very important that people in the world and in the second generation come to see and learn about this. So they do not forget."

So they do not forget.

I hoped that every country wouldn't have to go through this in order to learn the same lesson. But yet I knew that most of them had. America lost over six hundred thousand men and women in the Civil War, and that doesn't even count the deaths from slavery. Britain lost over two million in the two World Wars. And that is nothing in comparison to the Russian loss of twenty-five million during World War II alone, or the Holocaust that culminated in the murder of six million Jews. The numbers are staggering. We could choke on them, and yet new wars break out every day.

We break our hearts, and then we break our hearts again. I walked back to Kindness One and it felt like I had been on the bike for years. Everything in my body hurt; my soul was exhausted. I tried to remember that for every tragic story, for every killing field, there are a million more stories of kindness. Of people loving one another despite their differences. But I couldn't help but wonder: Could those kindnesses ever balance out the loss?

I returned to the pulsating city of Phnom Penh and found a place to stay for the night. I was exhausted from what I had seen, and I was ready to begin what was going to be the last leg of my Asian journey: a small trip across the Vietnamese border and then seventy miles to my final ship back to North America. I was heading to Canada, and then I would be riding down to LA.

I couldn't even fathom how quickly this was all happening. I had seen so much and I knew it would feel like only a brief whoosh of time before I would be waking up again in LA — Lina in the living room, checking her emails, Winston at the foot of my bed, or more likely, licking my face. And all of this — these moments standing in front of history, walking through the stories of other people's lives, driving across borders and traveling across oceans — all of this would be over.

And the one thing that would connect me

back to the people I had met and the places I had seen would be the gifts. Just as they had become the reason for this journey, so they would also be the greatest witness of it. The gifts would keep me in touch with Tony and Seng and Tchale. I would be emailing with Alex and Nasuh and Willy. All those lives and moments would be carried into my present. Now, I just had to get there.

The good people at the shipping company had offered to take me back to North America for free. It was the same generous company that had helped me across the Atlantic, and now it would be getting Kindness One and me home. I would spend a few days in Ho Chi Minh city while my bike was being prepared for the long trip across the Pacific. Together, we would take a ship back to North America, back to LA, back to Lina and Winston, and — deep breath — back *home.*

But God had different plans. Or what had become my new word for God — East Asian border guards.

I left Cambodia relatively easily, getting my passport stamped in record time — well, at least in comparison to *getting into* Cambodia. A representative from the shipping company had even come along to smooth over the process, as I was a bit worried after my entrance into Cambodia. The first step of the process went surprisingly well. Passport stamped. Visa viewed. The second part of the process went horribly wrong.

This is the part where you tell me that you know someone at the Vietnamese border crossing and I should have called you. Well, a little late, my friend. And even more than that, I'm not sure it would have worked. I wondered whether they would have let the president in had he dared to enter with a yellow motorbike. Because apparently, a yellow motorbike was right under an AK-47 in terms of dangerous items to allow into Vietnam. As soon as I pushed the bike up to the second checkpoint, he took one look at it and said in his best English, "Impossible for bike to Vietnam. Impossible."

But those words didn't faze me — at least not at first. I could see freedom a hundred fifty feet away, so I knew I was close. Plus, if I had become an expert at nothing else on this trip, it was rejection. I asked to speak with the chief. I was told to wait thirty minutes. I stepped outside of the crowded office, and then the weather turned, rain quickly drenched me as I fought against an onslaught of other travelers all trying to seek shelter within.

Finally, the chief came out. I was soaking wet. Kindness One was soaking wet. We needed some good news. He looked at the bike, and looked at my paper work, which I had managed to keep dry, and then repeated the words of his associates, "Impossible for bike to Vietnam, Englishman."

Well, he didn't have to add the Englishman bit, but that was okay. I would find someone else. Two people saying no was just the beginning. I'd keep going. I would go through every single border guard until I found the words I was looking for: "Greetings for bike to Vietnam, Englishman."

I asked to speak to the chief of all chiefs — the big chief. The current chief apparently didn't like this question, since he thrust my papers back into my hands and marched away. I waited, and then another man, who was tall and wide and looked like he should be the Head of Something, came out with four minions, including the last chap, who had gone to find him. The head chief looked at me like I was insane and shook his head as he gave the verdict, "You, inside Vietnam. Bike, back to Cambodia."

Things were now getting serious. So I decided that I would start crying. It had worked before. I figured the head chief and his four minions would budge once I hit my knees and started weeping. The only difference was that this time the tears were real. The head chief barked at me, "Come inside."

I must have been embarrassing him in front of the other travelers. I didn't mind. I was going to have a private audience with the chief. Once in his office, I went straight into the story. My wife, Lina. My three sons. My dog, Winston.

"I won't get there without my bike," I explained. "I don't have any money. Just my bike."

He squinted at me from across the table. Like others I had come across, he could not believe that an Englishman with a yellow motorbike would be doing this without any money.

"You are fine. You have visa," he explained as calmly as he could. "But the bike, it cannot come."

There was nothing more I could do. I persuaded them to place the bike in a container at the border and promised I would be back. All I knew was that in seven days, I would be getting on that ship to Canada, and I would be doing it with Kindness One in tow.

I found my way into the center of Ho Chi Minh, without my yellow hunk of magic, and was assured by Hao, my contact at the shipping company, that they would resolve it.

"Enjoy the sites and sounds of Vietnam," Hao told me. "And be sure to check your email."

No problem — that was an order I could follow. The best part in all of this was that I wouldn't need to worry about convincing anyone to buy gas for me!

My days in Ho Chi Minh were spent waiting for good news and doing what I had done in every other city along the way — I searched for food and friends and places to stay. I ended up begging my way into a hotel for one night, and the next I stayed with a street cleaner. My trusty computer was always at the ready, but still no news.

The container ship would soon be leaving for Canada, but Hao had told me not to worry. One afternoon, I decided to go out and find a bowl of noodles for lunch. Anything to take my mind off my quickly unraveling plans. I saw a girl in line in front of me and asked if she spoke English. She did and was impressed with my story. Enough to buy me lunch and hear more as we ate.

Vin explained to me that offering me lunch was not a rare act for her. "It's part of my nature," she told me. "I like to help people. Especially foreigners who are not familiar with our country."

She opened her arms wide as she exclaimed, "So I speak for the people, and I welcome you and host you."

If only the border guards had been so inviting.

"What are your dreams?" I asked Vin. "What do you dream about?"

She thought about it for a second. "I do dream that I can help people have a better life."

As we were finishing our lunch, she told me about a doctor she knew, "He believes in kindness, too. In helping people. This doctor he gives people their eyes back."

Okay. I was a little confused. "He helps the blind?"

"Yes, for poor people. With him, they can see." She thought about it before asking, "Would you like to meet this doctor?"

Twenty minutes later, after a terrifying trip on the back of Vin's scooter, we were at the clinic of the doctor.

We walked into the waiting room, which was filled with people. They were all visually impaired, some accompanied by a child or grandchild. The doctor came out to take back a new client, but Vin quickly went to him and explained where I was from and what I was doing.

He asked if we could wait while he attended to a few more patients for the day. As we sat in the waiting room, Vin translated various conversations with the people around us. I learned that many of them lived in rural communities, where access to doctors was difficult. I discovered that many of them weren't suffering from permanent blindness, but simply cataracts. In the West, cataract surgery was a very common procedure, but for these rural villagers, it was out of reach. Most of the patients expected to go blind by the end of their lives, despite the simple fix.

"But the surgery is so easy," I told Vin.

"Yes," she replied, shrugging her shoulders. "It's just hard for people to find doctor to do. They cannot afford."

Not long after, the doctor came and brought us into his office. Dr. Nguyen spoke English, which he had picked up while studying in England.

He explained his work as simply being a part of his community: "I think it's just a part of my job, helping the poor blind people to see again. Being blind is such a heavy burden for them and for their family."

The doctor's humility helped me set my own worries aside. Sure, Kindness One sat in lock up at the border, but what did that matter in comparison to this work? "It puts everything into perspective for me. That I saw all of those people upstairs who couldn't see when they came here and now they can," I shared.

The doctor gently shrugged and replied, "It is my job. It is my calling."

I remembered back to the first day I set foot in America, determined to cross it on only $5 a day. There I was — a grown man, who had once been the awkwardly shy kid in class — going up to anyone who would look in my direction, asking them for help, trying to plead a cause I wasn't so sure I believed in myself. Adventure had set me free. It was what made me feel a part of this collective life. It was *my calling.*

Though the doctor had studied abroad, he had decided to take what he had learned and bring it back to his own people. He had brought the adventure home. I wondered whether I might do the same. Or whether chance meetings like this might always call me away?

I motioned to Vin, saying, "Had you not been in that noodle shop today, I wouldn't have met you."

And then I turned to the doctor, "And had I not met Vin, I wouldn't have met you. I wouldn't have seen the amazing work that you are doing."

I smiled, realizing out loud, "One second difference, and none of us would have crossed paths. And here we are, sitting together."

Vin laughed, replying, "I think this came from your side first. If you didn't plan to be in Ho Chi Minh City, you could not see all of us here. So this came from you first."

She was right. Had my bike not been detained, had I not been stuck in Ho Chi Minh City for days, I wouldn't have met either of them. I wouldn't have seen the doctor's inspiring work, or met his wonderful patients, or made a new friend in Vin.

Suddenly I felt overwhelmed with emotion. Waiting for the bike. Meeting all these wonderful people, who just wanted to connect, to help, to love. Seeing how this man had realized that the best work didn't happen someplace else, but locally. I could feel my voice choking as I blurted out: "What I want to do is help pay for one hundred surgeries."

They both looked stunned. I think I was a little stunned as well. In America, one hundred surgeries would have been very expensive, indeed. What had I done? Surely this would bankrupt me.

Fortunately, I soon found out that the cost of the surgery in Vietnam was far more reasonable.

The doctor thanked me, still a little in shock from my offer. "We are very, very happy when we see kind people like you, who are giving help to the poor people. I also think if you do that, you also feel happy."

Vin added, "I wish you have a long life and that you help more people around the world."

As I walked out of the clinic, Vin's words echoed in my ears: "I hope you help more people around the world." I wondered if this trip were just the beginning. Just as I had loved connecting with strangers while crossing America a few years before, now, I had found another love, another calling: helping others fulfill their dreams. A lofty goal, I know, but I like lofty goals.

Should all that stop after I returned home to LA? Maybe I would be taking what I learned from this journey and finding new ways to continue it — not only across the world, but also at home.

I continued walking through the city and decided that if ever there were a time for karma to return to me, now would be it. I went into an Internet café and pulled out my computer, feeling like a gambler at the slot machine in Vegas. Come on, Vietnam! What I found was nothing. Well, something, but nothing good. It was another email from my friends at the shipping company. They still weren't able to get the Vietnamese to sign off on releasing my bike.

I shut down the computer and thought long and hard, and then I opened it back up and went to Google. I typed in six very important words: US Embassy Ho Chi Minh City.

It was time to bring in the Americans.

Now why not go to your own people, you might ask? First, for logistics — the bike was a registered American "citizen." And second, I had a feeling that no one likes getting a call from the US embassy.

After finagling a place to stay with some friendly backpackers (Canadians, in fact!), I woke up the next morning and met with a representative at the American embassy. They looked at my documents, heard my plea (no crying or lying this time), and promised to look into it.

"I am trying to get on a boat in four days," I explained.

The American agent was at least more

friendly than the border guards, but he was not much more optimistic. He looked at my documents again as he murmured, "Four days?"

Finally, he looked up. "That might take a miracle, Mr. Logo-the-tis."

I walked out, stunned. I thought if anyone could help, it would be the US embassy, and now even they were talking about miracles. I had already been praying for a miracle. What I needed was some good, old-fashioned diplomatic strong-arming.

I didn't even notice where I was going as I walked down the streets of Ho Chi Minh City, frustration boiling up inside me — the anger, the pain, the exhaustion of being trapped in a foreign land, with no clear passage home.

I thought back to when I was riding through Cambodia, believing I was only days away from boarding the ship that would take me back to my adopted continent, and now it felt like I would be trapped in Ho Chi Minh City indefinitely. Talk about the walls closing in. I would like to think that I wasn't talking to myself (I was) when an older man approached me. He was dressed in a modern suit, and I could tell by the clean haircut and shined shoes that he was probably someone kind of important.

He had stepped out of the imposing wooden doors of the Ho Chi Min City opera house and walked right up to me. I feared he was going to tell me to get off the marble steps but instead he asked me with a deep concern, "You are okay, Mister?"

I was most certainly not okay.

It's one thing to be blathering on to yourself, but it's an entirely different thing when your audience includes an elderly gentleman in a business suit.

"No, I'm fine," I explained. "I'm just having a minor meltdown. I've found myself stuck in Ho Chi Minh City. Which has been lovely really, but . . ."

He stared at me, waiting for something else.

Finally, I confessed, "I'm just tired."

"Yes, life can do this to us."

His sympathy made me relax a bit, enough to explain my journey.

"And how perfect," he replied, laughing. "It has brought you here to our opera house."

"Well, not in the best condition," I admitted before telling him about my journey.

He smiled at me warmly, reminding me of the fatherly concern of Filipo in Italy. He seemed to know how fraught long days can feel.

"Are you here tonight?" Bao asked me. I looked up. Removed from my frustration for a moment, I hoped he might offer me a meal or a place to stay.

"Yes," I quickly replied.

"Then maybe we make your night better. Would you like to come and see the opera?" he offered.

I felt like I was back in India, suddenly being asked to a karate match while Kindness One leaked in the background. But I figured no one was going to kick me in the face at the opera.

That night I arrived and sat in my seat, wearing the same shabby clothes that had accompanied me the whole trip. I had discovered upon going into the opera house to retrieve my ticket that it was the director himself who had invited me. At the intermission, Bao came up and asked me if I would be interested in joining the performers on stage.

Joining the performers on stage? Surely this man wasn't real.

He *was* real, and soon I found myself standing on stage in front of an audience of hundreds. You cannot make this stuff up.

During the last ten minutes of the show, they gave me a set of drums and allowed me to become a part of the performance.

For those ten minutes, I poured everything I had into those drums — the exhaustion, the joy, the fears, the kindness, the cry for home, and the exhilaration that had reverberated throughout my journey. I had never been much of a musician (as Tchale and Finesse could certainly attest), but in that moment, it didn't matter. I wasn't just banging away on some drums, I was telling a story, one that I hoped might end well — or at the very least, would end with me getting out of Nam.

As I came out to give my bow, people started enthusiastically clapping for me. And it hit me.

More than anything else, the most important thing we need is to be seen by others. It wasn't just the fuel for greatness; it was part of the foundation of survival. I thought back to Seng, alone in her rickety house, with no one watching out for her. Perhaps loneliness is the most fatal disease. We all need to feel acknowledged by those around us. We need to be seen. And we also need to be able to see others. Doctor Nguyen was restoring sight, but more than just fixing their vision, he was acknowledging their right to have a dignified place in this world.

And in many ways, through my gifts, I was also trying to do just that. If nothing else, I wanted to acknowledge their existence, their struggle. Because life is hard. And sometimes it brings us to our knees. We need someone to find us on the opera steps, to remind us that no matter how desperate or terrifying or mundane our lives might become, we shouldn't lose sight of the music around us. In fact, it just means we have to play louder, play so loudly that we drown out the pain or fear, or even the impossible border guards waging war against yellow motorbikes!

For so many years, I hadn't felt seen, and yet here I was at the Ho Chi Minh City Opera House, bowing before an applauding audience — because sometimes it's also the big moments.

CHAPTER TWELVE

"There is no psychiatrist in the world like
a puppy licking your face."
— Ben Williams

I got the call at seven in the morning: "The ambassador will see you today."

Upon arriving at the consulate, however, I discovered that I would not actually be meeting with the ambassador, himself. Instead, an appointment had been arranged with a consulate official that worked in customs. Sounded just as good to me.

After the call, I headed over to the official's office to find out just what miracles they had in store for me. He asked if I had all my documents with me. I did — my bike's registration, the carnet, and other records that basically vouched for my status as a really good guy and not someone who was part of an underground terrorist network.

The official then handed them to his assistant and asked that they be photocopied. He turned to me and explained: "I can't make you any promises, but we'll see what we can do."

As the official and I waited for the assistant to return, he tried to explain the tricky little Vietnamese customs law that had kept Kindness One locked in solitary confinement for the better part of the week: You could only bring in items that you could literally carry. Unless that item was new. But Kindness One was far from new, and there was no way I could carry it.

Not long after, the official seemed concerned that his assistant had not returned. He called him back in the office and asked for the documents. The assistant cocked his head: "The documents?"

Oh, shit.

"Yes," the official tried quite valiantly to keep his cool. "The documents?"

"Oh," his assistant replied nonchalantly, "I shredded those."

Yes, you heard that right. I mean, at the time, the official and I both doubted our hearing, but what the assistant had said was true. He had shredded all of my most important documents. In the process he had actually done me an enormous favor —

though I certainly didn't know that then. I could barely hear the official talking as he made apologies, promises, and tried desperately not to dress down his hapless underling, who was now only beginning to realize his error. Or should I say, the magnitude of his error.

I left the embassy in a fog of desperation, shock clinging to me. All week Hao had been saying, "Don't worry, Leon. Everything is going to be okay."

But Hao was wrong. Everything was not going to be okay.

I went back to the apartment where I had found shelter the last two nights and called Lina. I was going to have to start coming up with other ways out of Vietnam. I was going to have to prepare myself for leaving behind Kindness One, and returning home . . . by plane.

"Leon, there could be far worse fates," Lina tried to comfort me.

"Name one," I tersely replied.

"You could be not coming home at all. You could have gotten hurt on the road. Or worse."

I knew she was right, but still, I had begun to create a new dream in my head: an image of me riding back into Los Angeles on Kindness One. The prodigal boyfriend returning home.

"You'll come home however you're supposed to," Lina continued. "Remember sometimes the universe sends a rainstorm so we don't drive into the tornado."

Who knew my girlfriend was a direct descendant of Mother Teresa?

I went to bed and prepared myself for another day of stormy weather.

The next day, I got another call from the consulate: Calls were being made, papers were being drawn, I should plan to head back to the border the next day to try to claim Kindness One. If I could have run to the consulate and kissed that assistant myself, I would have. Because here is the other side of kindness — though happiness cannot be bartered, to a certain extent, kindness can. Because of the documents mishap, the official likely felt he, how shall I put it, "owed me one." And that tradeoff might just have been Kindness One's only way out of Vietnam.

I returned to the guard who had denied me only days before.

The guard looked down at my paperwork and nodded: "Hold on."

Hold on. Okay, that I could do. I had been doing it for five days, so what were a few more moments? He went and spoke with the chief, who had been telling me no for days on end — via email, via telephone, and in person. The men nodded and looked gruffly in my direction.

The guard came back, and replied without smiling, "You take bike now."

"Into Vietnam?" I asked.

He nodded again, as though this were not a big deal. As though foreigners with vintage yellow bikes did this every day. He told me to go to the container where Kindness One was being held.

Never had I been so happy to have annoyed an entire country.

I had learned by that point that things are never easy at border crossings. After Hao drove me back to where Kindness One was being detained, we soon found out a rather unfortunate slice of information. After speaking further with the Vietnamese border authorities, we discovered that I could have the bike, but I would not be allowed to ride it in Vietnam.

I could have the bike, but I would not be allowed to ride it in Vietnam?

The magic of yellowness had finally met its match. Or had it? Because where there are problems, there are solutions. If only I could find a solution before having a heart attack in my late thirties.

I would need to have the bike transported in a sealed container to the port, seventy miles away.

Sensing my growing desperation, Hao came to the rescue and offered to arrange a truck to take Kindness One to the port. I accepted. Blood pressure reduced. Hope increased. When the truck showed up, however, we realized it was missing one very important detail: a ramp. As in, the ramp we needed to wheel the bike into the back of the truck. After some thought, I came up with the only plan that made any sense — though, as you will see, it actually made no sense. We would lift the bike *into* the truck. Yes, we would lift a nearly one-ton bike into the back of a Vietnamese truck.

Madness?

Yes.

But also our only option.

There was only the truck driver, Hao, and myself. The three of us stood there, looking back and forth from the bike to the truck. There was no way we were going to be able to pull it off alone, so I started recruiting the porters who worked at the border, asking them for help. By now, my little one-ton(ish) bike and I had become quite famous, or rather, infamous. I think the border guards would have paid to get me out of there. I quickly gathered nine people, and we put the plan in motion.

Our first attempt didn't go so well. The bike tilted back and forth as the group tried to get it balanced. Already I had become known as the biggest pain in the ass this side of the Vietnamese border. As the porters shot me dirty looks trying to launch my bike into the back of the truck, I knew my time in Vietnam was running out. Finally, we found our stride, and Kindness One was bound for the nearby port.

We had done it. I was literally carrying Kindness One into Vietnam. Now why didn't I think of this at the beginning?

Getting Kindess One into Vietnam should have only taken seven hours; instead, it had taken nearly seven days, but I didn't mind. I had explored the city, staying with business executives and street cleaners, kitchen cooks and opera directors. I had avoided the tornado, and in turn, I had walked through a rainstorm of kindness. For every rough moment at the border, I had experienced the generosity of the Vietnamese people ten-fold, not to mention the incredible efforts of the American consulate.

The next day, I arrived at the port and saw the ship that would take Kindness One across the vast blue ocean that separated us from North America and our destination of Vancouver, Canada. I stepped on the ship and looked out at the city. I was going home.

In India, I was given a copy of Gregory David Roberts' *Shantaram*, a book about a man who lives mired in the darker side of Bombay. I was lying in my bunk on the cargo ship when I read the first paragraph (and, admittedly, the only part I read): *"It took me a long time and most of the world to learn what I know about love and fate and the choices we make, but the heart of it came to me in an instant . . . that freedom is a universe of possibility."*

I got up and walked outside for some fresh air. A cool breeze lapped in across the ocean as I pulled my jacket tighter. No matter how hard some of the days on the road had been, no matter how painful it was to see the lives of those who had much less, no matter how I might have longed for home or wished I could have done better, done more, been more, I knew that this journey had been born of that freedom. The freedom to kiss my girlfriend good-bye, get on Kindness One, and drive across the world. I knew that not everyone lives in the same freedom, but maybe it isn't just a matter of having enough resources or time or effort or talent. Maybe it's just realizing that freedom is ours for the taking. As is possibility. As is living your dream.

Nineteen days later, I walked off the ship into the Vancouver port and was quickly reminded of another quote: "The most dangerous moment comes with victory in sight."

Napoleon said that, and he knew about this sort of thing. As the frigid air of a Canadian winter hit me in the face, I realized that while victory might have been in sight, it wasn't yet mine. Because I quickly realized that Canada is not warm.

You see, I may have left Los Angeles during the summer months and followed the sun around the world, but I had returned to North America in the winter.

All I had was my threadbare red jacket, which I had been wearing in the summer months, and a raggedy old pullover. And to make matters worse, I had arrived during a particularly chilly cold snap. Everyone I met was talking about it, including the crew, who looked at me incredulously as I climbed on Kindness One and bid them farewell in the freezing winds. By the time I arrived in the center of the city, I was convinced that I had frostbite. I probably did have frostbite. I knew where frostbite could lead — death.

And let's face it, I hadn't made it around the world, through Europe, the Middle East, Asia, and across three major oceans to die of frostbite in Vancouver.

I stumbled into a restaurant, and when the owners saw me they knew something was wrong. After explaining my story, the first thing they did was place me next to a fire. The second thing they did was feed me. The third thing they did was feed me some more.

Paul and Maureen had owned their restaurant for thirty years, but they seemed more intent to tell me about the Canadian Rockies.

"You've never been?" Maureen asked me with a shocked tone as she served me another bowl of soup. I could barely speak, so I just shook my head as my shaky spoon moved to my mouth.

"Oh, Leon! You've got to go," Maureen cried in response.

"Truly the most beautiful thing you've ever seen," Paul added.

I nodded again, wondering how they could boast about cold mountain air while I was still trying to defrost from it. But boast they did. They told me about the snow-covered mountains, skiing, nature, and rogue bears.

I must admit that I wasn't really listening. I was eating and getting as close to the fire as I could without jumping in it.

I explained that I would love to visit the Rockies, hoping my enthusiasm would quell them. And then I added that I was looking for a place to stay for the night.

"Well, we have our in-laws in town," Paul began.

"Oh, I'm sorry hon," Maureen seemed genuinely disappointed that they couldn't help. "Don't you know anyone in Vancouver?"

At no other point on this trip had I reached out to someone I knew. I maintained my commitment to strangers, but I did know someone in Vancouver, or rather I knew of her. Lina's 102-year-old great-grandmother lived alone in the Canadian city. When Lina found out the ship would be taking me there, she had offered to call her Nana, explaining that the centenarian would be overjoyed to have me visit. She nudged, "I mean if you're trying to be kind, and all, why not be kind to a 102-year-old lady?"

I had taken down the number, but only to be nice. But now, faced with going out in the blustery cold, searching for a warm home with nothing but this lightweight jacket to keep me alive, Lina's Nana seemed like the perfect prospect. Maureen loaned me their phone, and I found out that Nora, Lina's great-grandmother, had heard about my trip.

"Of course you can stay, Leon," she replied. "I was hoping you would call."

The only problem with going to Nora's was that I would have to go outside again. In the cold. With no more clothes than I had before. Thankfully, it turned out her house was only twenty minutes away. I could drive twenty minutes.

Or I thought I could drive twenty minutes. Halfway there, I had to stop. Gusts of cold air were blowing in my face, the wind chill making it feel like ten below. I stopped at a gas station and found someone kind enough to buy me some gas. Very helpful. But what was even more helpful was his offer to buy me some gloves and a full face mask!! I had been wearing a now worn-out pair of yellow gloves for most of my journey, but they were most certainly not Canadian-proof.

I arrived at Nora's in full face mask and winter gloves. She answered the door in a stylish red jacket and quickly ushered me in.

"Oh dear, Leon," she fussed. "You must be freezing."

She initially reminded me of Kay, Willy's friend in Colorado, but as soon as I saw a family photo in the foyer, which included my beautiful girlfriend, she also reminded me of Lina.

After meeting her friend John, who was also visiting her, I told Nora how happy I was to be there, and not just because she was Lina's Nana. I told her, "It's quite an honor to be in the presence of someone who's lived so long."

"I never thought I'd live this long," she laughed.

John added, smiling in Nora's direction, "I'm sticking close to her because I'll want some of that to rub off on me."

"How old are *you*?" I asked John.

"Well, I'm 88."

Nora winked, "He's a spring chicken!"

Nora was born in 1911, one year before the Titanic sank. Three years before the outbreak of World War I. When Nora was born, William Taft was the president of America. Now it was President Barack Obama. In 1911, African Americans weren't even allowed to vote.

Nora, John, and I began to talk about the moments from the last century. I was in awe of these two people who had seen so much history, and were still here to talk about it.

We made our way all the way up to the 1960s, when we began discussing the moon landing. I was born long after that fateful day, but I still remember seeing the photos of those first steps and wondering how such a thing had occurred. The idea that man could actually be blasted into space was of course nearly miraculous, but then to imagine what Neil Armstrong must have felt in that moment — caught between the silence of the moon and the great big planet down below watching him. I asked John and Nora what that moment was like for them.

John said, "It was something that . . . they talked about it for so long that when it finally happened, I still didn't believe it. But when I saw the picture of them landing on the moon, I'll tell you, it was quite an event."

Sometimes dreams are like that. We talk about them for a long time before they can happen. Sometimes we are the only people left who still believe that they will. And when your dream is to go to the moon. Well, that takes a lot of talking.

I remembered *The Odyssey*. At the end of the journey, only Odysseus believes he will make it home. So many distractions, so many challenges, and yet he knows that one day, he will return to Ithaca.

I imagined the odyssey that first took

those three men to the moon was no different. People had been looking up at that luminous rock for thousands and thousands of years, and in 1969, the two people sitting in front of me (along with many other millions) had watched it all happen on television.

And then we talked about my own odyssey. All the places I had visited and people I had met. I realized as I was describing my trip to Bhutan that it didn't even feel real. It felt like a dream I had had. Not something I had actually lived.

"And now I'm heading home," I told them. The words just as strange as the trip I had explained.

"Well, that's the real adventure, isn't it?" Nora asked.

"Yes, it is," I admitted, still wondering what life would be like upon my return. I told Nora and John about how much I learned from the people I had met, and then I asked Nora, "So if there is one thing you could teach me about life. What would it be?"

She smiled gently and put her hand on my arm, "Love."

I wasn't sure if that was a command, or just the whole reason for being here. Or maybe both.

Nora had shoulder-length hair that she brushed across her head and steely blue eyes that sparkled. She seemed to read my mind as she explained, "Surround yourself with love."

In many ways, what the ocean was to Odysseus, love had been to me. I had been sailing through it this whole trip. Rocked by it at some points, but carried by it for most of the journey. John offered me a heavy jacket he had in his truck. After feeding me a warm meal, Nora told me that I could sleep as much as I wanted the next day. That is love. I wondered if I could sustain the one I had back home.

But first, it was time to go to the Rockies. I had my new warm jacket in hand, and had gotten yet another earful from John and Nora the night before about the beauty of Canada's mountains. Again the words from *Shantaram* echoed in my mind, "Freedom is a universe of possibility."

Now if Lina had known that, just as I was so close to home, I had decided to head north, in the other direction, I am sure she would have shaken her head, and whispered, "Running." But my whole journey had been dictated by such detours — people guiding my path for me, often diverting my itinerary as I moved from city to city. I had been sold on the fabled mountain range, so off I went to Whistler, in the Canadian Rockies.

The full face mask. The new coat. The new gloves. Unfortunately, they were all very nice accessories, but not very helpful ones. The ride up to Whistler was extraordinarily beautiful but absolute hell for my face and brain, which was close to a critical malfunction. After a few hours, I finally reached the famed mountains, my lips practically frozen together. I needed to find a place to stay. I left Kindness One, hoping it wouldn't freeze to death while I searched for warmth. So far Kindness One had never had to deal with the cold.

I asked the many tourists who populated the ski resort at that time of year for a place to stay, but it appeared there was no room for me. I finally decided to try a hotel. I had found that it was at the moment when I was closest to giving up, that I usually found my next miracle. I was getting used to this rodeo by now.

After recounting my journey across earth, the hotel manager offered me a room for the night. And not just any room. I was living in luxury for the day. I had my own fire, my own TV, my own hot running water. I don't think I had slept better the whole journey. Comfortable beds. Clean sheets.

Peace and quiet. I dreamed of my bed back home. I thought of Odysseus returning home to his love, to the life he had left behind. I wondered if my own life had changed much. Would I be going back to the same place? Would I be the same man? Or would I be a stranger in my own home?

The next morning, I took a walk around the village. Everyone had been right. The place was gorgeous. High mountains topped with snow, the crisp and brilliant air of a beautiful day — even the sun shone across the snowy landscape, a bright kaleidoscope of white and silver reflecting back the sun's rays. Just as nature had done so many times before, it restored my faith. Much like on that first day driving to Vegas, I felt like I was exactly where I was supposed to be.

As I was walking through the Olympic village, site of the 2010 winter games, I bumped into a dog. Or should I say a dog bumped into me.

I quickly found out from Growler's owner, Sophie, that he was adopted from a nearby shelter.

I sometimes say if you can't love a human, love a dog.

So I decided to visit the shelter in honor of the dog who made me who I am.

I got Winston when he was only twelve

weeks old. He is now twelve years old. We have a special bond, a bond that in many ways preceded my ability to truly connect with my fellow humans. Don't get me wrong. I have always loved people, but I didn't really know how to reach out to them, how to show them that I wasn't afraid and that they didn't need to be either. And then I got Winston.

I had never loved something so unconditionally before. In fact, I have even had a couple of love interests accuse me of loving him more, but what I eventually came to realize was that Winston was teaching me how to love, period. To always see the best in people, to believe in them, to be thrilled just because they walked through the door. I heard someone once say that dogs only live for part of our lives. But we are their whole life.

I walked into the shelter ready to meet some of the wonderful dogs whose forever homes I hoped were just around the corner. Angie was a volunteer from South Africa who worked at the shelter and completely understood my connection with our furry little friends.

"They really have a way of creeping into our hearts, don't they?" she asked.

Sadly, many dogs don't get the lives they

deserve. Angie told me, "We get countless dogs that have been hit by cars or just completely abandoned. They come in like racks of bones and just in terrible shape. But we do our best to help them out."

Angie and I walked to the kennel. I was quickly overwhelmed by the volume of barking dogs and the unmistakable odor of animals living in close quarters. Angie introduced me to a dog named Mia, who had been tied to the back of a pickup truck and dragged. Nearly to her death.

They had just found her a foster home that day. And they had already performed critical surgeries on her. Angie explained as we met Mia, "The thing is, we've had dogs that have had to have amputations. They've had such traumatic previous lives. And yet they still learn to love again."

If only all of us could remember that lesson — that even in the darkest hours, when our dreams have been dashed or our hearts broken, we can all learn to love again. Whether it's a person, a dog, or a dream, it's the resiliency of love that keeps us alive.

I knew that was what Winston had done for me. He had saved me. Maybe it wasn't about going to a shelter to rescue a dog; maybe it was about going to a shelter to be rescued, yourself.

I hadn't intended to come to Whistler, and I doubt when people told me to go see the Rockies, they thought I would spend most of my day at a dog shelter.

I explained to Angie as we walked around the kennel, "As I told you, I have a dog, Winston Churchill, and the thought of my dog being out on the streets, cold, with nowhere to sleep and no food and having you come and help him really touches me. The number of dogs and cats that you've helped and lives that you've changed are pretty inspirational."

Angie and I continued talking as she worked. All of my gifts thus far had been given to people, but I realized that if I could offer the shelter one thing, it would be to give their current dogs the best home possible.

As Angie put a young puppy back in its kennel, I told her about my journey and about the gifts. She stopped what she was doing to listen as I continued, "And I want to help you too. And I think, well the way I can do that is to restock the entire facility with new beds, medicine, toys, collars, anything that the dogs need, anything that you need to make the dogs happier and to get a forever home quicker."

Angie locked the kennel and looked at me

in shock, "Really, Leon?"

"Really. Anything."

She shook her head before replying, "If dogs could talk —"

I laughed, interrupting her, "They'd probably ask for more food."

"Well, that's for sure," she agreed before continuing, her eyes lighting up as spoke. "But they'd also say thank you, so I'll do it for them. Thank you."

When Odysseus finally arrived home, dressed in the clothes of a beggar, no one recognized him, not even his wife, Penelope. Nope, the only one who did know it was him was his dog, Argos. Twenty years, Odysseus was gone (making my few months look like a weekend getaway), and yet when he returned, his dog was still waiting for him, wanting nothing more than to lick his face and offer his enduring love.

As I left Whistler, I knew that I was going to my forever home, too. I had some amazing stories to tell Winston when I got there. He would be proud.

CHAPTER THIRTEEN

"A man travels the world over
in search of what he needs
and returns home to find it."
— George A. Moore

I drove up to the American border. I closed
my eyes and breathed in deep. So many long
and weary roads were behind me. So many
nights, I had closed my eyes and still could
see the white lines in the middle of the road
as though they were painted on the inside
of my eyelids. And here I was — the final
frontier. Or at least the final border. And
this time, I knew we would have no problems getting across. I had my green card in
my pocket, the un-shredded pieces of Kindness One's American registration papers
(which had caused so much trouble in
Asia), and one straight road home, right
into the heart of LA.

My little magic hunk of yellowness was

nearing the end of its epic journey, as was its captain. I was functioning purely on adrenaline. Maybe I didn't realize it until much later, but I had been functioning on adrenaline for the bulk of my trip: from riding a motorbike on narrow mountain passes, to negotiating every day for food and places to stay. As much as this journey had been sponsored by kindness, it had been powered by adrenaline.

As I reached the US border, I was out of that neurobiological fuel. I handed the guard my papers, and after quickly looking them over, he waved me through. I drove half a mile down the road and then pulled over.

Out of earshot of the border patrol, I jumped off Kindness One and began to shout. I had made it. I had made it across the border. I had made it across the world. I was going to make it home. I mean, sure, home was just over one thousand miles away, but that was close enough. I knelt down on American soil and kissed the ground. I had made it.

I had my face mask, my warm winter jacket from John, and my Canadian-proof gloves, but it was still freezing. For that moment, however, even the winter chill couldn't stop me. The same warmth that had flooded me on that day on Hollywood Boulevard flooded me again. I had left my house so many months before with only a slight sense of the dream I had wanted to fulfill. I would drive across the world on a yellow motorbike with no money for food, gas, or lodging. I would rely on the kindness of others, and would give some of those others a gift to fulfill their own dreams. And sure, yes, I did all that, but what I didn't realize is that I was giving myself the biggest gift of all. Because though Willy and Tony and Finesse and Tchale and Nasuh and Dilip and Angie might have all received something from my journey, what *I* received was the ability to pay attention to *their* journeys, to connect to *their* lives. It was like that Salman Rushdie quote, "To understand just one life, you must swallow the world."

I got back on my bike and began my ride through the majestic beauty of northern Washington. There are moments in your life when suddenly it feels like you can look back and see how every dot was connected — how one moment led to the next, how this person led you to that experience, or how that experience led you to this person. As I drove through the mountains, I could see that fabric of time linking me back to one of those early mentors who taught me how to believe.

Mr. Martin was a football coach at my high school, and I was an avid football player in my early days. The game was an escape from my problems at home and at school. I would get lost in the match . . . even if I only knew how to play one position.

I had always been a goalkeeper. Now for those of you who don't know, when the time is right, the goalkeeper can be a critical position, but for most of the game, you just stand there and wait. And wait. And wait some more. I would watch as my brother played striker, darting across the field, scoring goals and basking in the afterglow of praise and recognition.

I had always wanted to be a striker, like my successful older brother, but "middle-child syndrome" had kept me from risking failure. And then one day something inside me snapped, and I raised my hand. I asked to play striker. I wanted to be the one to score the goals . . . and I thought I would finally get my glory.

It didn't quite work out that way.

I was awful. And I never played striker again.

Three years later, I switched schools and

met Mr. Martin. Mr. Martin was a football coach not because he was paid to be one, but because he loved it. He loved the game. He knew that sports could bring out the best in us. He was a London taxi driver by profession, and I imagine he met people of all walks of life in his work. Maybe that's what made him so compassionate. He had gotten to know so many people, he knew without ever saying much that each life has its potential — and needs someone to nurture it.

Under his tutelage, I got up the courage to ask to play striker again. After the fifth game in which I failed to score, Mr. Martin took me aside and he said, "Do you believe in yourself? Be honest."

I looked down at my cleats, unsure how to respond because I was ashamed of the answer. Finally, I looked up, trying not to lock eyes with him, as I admitted quietly, "Not really."

He bent down so that I couldn't avoid his stare, and he said, "That's why you can't score."

And then his voice softened to a whisper as he added, "I believe in you."

He walked off, and I could hear his words echoing in my soul. It was all I needed really, just that one person to unlock that

319

part of me that feared I would never amount to much. I went out that afternoon, and I scored. That year, I went on to be the top striker for my team. Three years later, I was the top scorer for my college. And years later, I believed that I could make it around the world on nothing but kindness. Because one man's kind words on a rainy afternoon in a sock-filled locker room had changed everything. Like Dr. Mann before him, his words might have been one of the first gifts that led to all the others. Because it took someone else to believe in *me* for me to believe in someone else.

The sun was beginning to lower against the wintery sky of Washington, and still all those years later, I could hear Mr. Martin's words: *I believe in you.* The night before, I had stayed with a college student in his dorm room, actually on the floor of his dorm room, where we spent a better part of the night talking about the trip that had led me there. He was so enthralled by what I had done that I asked him if he ever hoped to travel.

"I'd like to," Ryan started, but then he explained. "But I'm on scholarship, and I don't know. I don't know how I'll ever get that chance."

The people of the world had given me a

chance. They had unlocked the part of me that didn't believe it could ever happen, and I realized as I drove through the deepening cold of an Oregon winter afternoon, that it was my turn to give that chance to someone else.

That morning, as I left Ryan, I told him, "If you believe in something hard enough, I find you can do almost anything." I felt Mr. Martin's words ricocheting across time, forever altering the course of one young man's life by giving him permission to dream, and now, I hoped, offering the same to another.

That night as I drove into the town of Eugene, I could feel Los Angeles drawing closer. I managed to meet a married couple who offered to put me up for the night. Bill and Melissa had been married for sixty-three years after a chance meeting in the late 1940s.

As we sat down that night, I asked how they had done it.

Bill looked over at his wife, "We're best friends."

I nodded, still unsure if that were enough. "Do you have a wife, Leon?" Melissa asked, squinting toward my hand to look for a ring.

"No," I smiled. "I have a girlfriend who wants to be a wife, though."

"Ohhhh," they said in unison.

Melissa thought about it before answering, "You know, when you're young, you think that it's just about you. You think that your happiness is what matters most, but I think as you get older you realize that it's the happiness of the people you love that will bring you the most joy."

I had seen that in all the relationships I had experienced on the road. I knew that giving joy brought joy, and yet something in me still balked at how to do that in my own home.

Bill nodded at what his wife said, "Don't worry Leon. Sometimes the success of a relationship has as much to do with how much it can handle as it does with how much you give it."

Melissa laughed, "I guess that makes us pretty indestructible."

In the morning, Bill came out to Kindness One and said, "I wish I had done what you are doing, keep traveling."

I laughed, "It's not the easiest on relationships."

"No, I doubt it is. But if you're with the right person, they'll always want to see you follow your dreams."

I knew that to keep traveling like this meant I would have to face the road alone.

If I wanted to travel the road that Bill had traversed with Melissa, I might need to stay home a bit more. I spent the next days riding across a wintery Oregon and into Northern California. My fingers were sore; my face was frozen. Even as signs began to appear announcing the miles until Los Angeles, I feared I would never make it. Never in my life had I so badly wanted to see Lina. I wanted to see Winston, and as the words subtly pounded themselves into my head, I realized that I wanted to go home.

And then I freaked out. Like, *really* freaked out.

I found myself in the early morning fog of Big Sur only 335 miles from home, and you can call it cold feet or spent nerves or whatever it might have been, but suddenly, I felt absolutely overwhelmed by the question that had plagued me this whole trip: could I go home and still live this adventure? Could I be a good partner and still connect to so many people across the world? I didn't want to be limited by domesticity, and yet at the same time, I didn't want to be untethered by adventure. I wanted both! I pulled over on the side of the highway, in the middle of the Redwoods. And there, right beside me, was a monastery. I guess

God was feeling bold today. Now, you could say it was a sign, but I'm pretty sure I'm not supposed to be a monk. Pretty sure. Okay, yes, thought about it: I'm sure.

The monastery was for the Brotherhood of St. Francis of Assisi, patron saint of animals and lost travelers along Highway One. Even though it was early, I left Kindness One on the side of the road and walked onto their property. Down at the edge was a bubbling brook. I looked around but didn't see anyone. I figured if ever there was a day to get arrested sneaking into a monastery, this was it.

I sat down by the water and tried to breathe. I didn't see the monk at first. I'm still not sure if he was there when I sat down or appeared after I did, but not five feet from me, there he was, standing at the edge of the water.

"I'm so sorry," I began. "I didn't know if this was open or —"

"It's always open, my son," the monk replied, echoing the man in the Indian ashram. He wasn't much older than I was, but with his heavy beard, he looked like he could have been my father.

"I just needed to think," I told the monk.

The monk sat down on a log not far from the water. "This is a good place for that.

What's on your mind?"

I don't suggest you open that can of worms . . .

But he had, and as I told him about my journey, about heading home, I could see his eyes grow brighter, I could see that my story was inspiring *him.*

"The world is filled with exciting places. As I am sure you have seen."

"I've seen a lot of them," I agreed.

"But the place we are often most needed isn't across the world. We're needed right here."

"Yeah, I'm beginning to realize that."

Finally, he said, "You know, we don't always have to leave home to find adventure."

"Don't we?" I asked.

"It just depends on what you do with your time at home," he stood up, and I began to worry that I was boring him. "My friend, this world is filled with possibility. Don't be limited by your old ideas of it. Let yourself live the lessons you learned. Teach them to others, and you'll find that's probably more adventurous than anything you've ever done."

"But what does that mean?" I asked, still lost in my anxiety over the approaching 335 miles.

The monk laughed, "I don't know, son. You get to decide the best way to share this journey. Just remember, sometimes it's about committing to people's hearts as well as their dreams."

Bells began to ring in the distance as the monk, whose name I never caught, said, "Morning prayers."

He was walking away by the time I thought to say thank you.

I began to think again about Mr. Martin and Ryan. I thought about all the people I had met along the way, who had said, "Wow, I wish I could do what you're doing," and I realized that this journey had to continue.

Now, now, don't worry. I am not about to do this again! Rather, it was time that someone else should. The journey couldn't stop with me. It needed to continue with a new person at its lead.

I walked out of the monastery, looking back at the quiet and peace of the monk's life. It had its draws, but I'm afraid not enough adrenaline for this chap. I got back on my bike and continued down Highway One, driving past Hearst Castle, where I could see a zeal of zebras standing in the distance, vestiges from when William Randolph Hearst had turned his grand terrain into a nature reserve. And that's when it hit me: I was going to give one final gift.

I pulled over at the next gas station and asked someone for a quarter. I had an important call to make. I waited as the phone rang, hoping to hear a voice on the other end.

"Hello?" the man answered.

My heart soared, "Dwight?"

Yes, Dwight, the first man to give me a tank of gas on Hollywood Boulevard, the man who had enabled me to start this entire journey. I had collected most of the names and emails and numbers of those who helped me along the way. I knew it was going to come in handy. On this one, I wasn't wrong.

I found my way back to Los Angeles, entering the city in a snarl of traffic, LA's typical greeting. Dwight had agreed to meet me for coffee that afternoon, though he was reasonably confused.

I told him that I wanted to meet up with him and give him a ride in Kindness One. I told him that he was the first person who helped me, so I wanted to thank him. What he didn't know was that my gratitude came with a gift.

We took a little joyride through LA. As we winded across town, fighting traffic against the hot winter weather and the constant welcome of palm trees, I was happy to hear the sounds of home. I drove us through Hollywood, down Sunset Boulevard, and up to the Griffith Park Observatory.

For those of you who are not familiar with Los Angeles, the observatory overlooks all of the city. It stands perched at the top of one of the tallest peaks of the Hollywood Hills, a smooth white dome looking down upon all the magic and dysfunction that is my adopted city. And it felt like the perfect place to keep this journey alive.

As Dwight and I drove up to the famed building, I did my final illegal act and drove the bike, right next to the edge of the cliff overlooking the great city of Los Angeles. We pulled over to a quiet, dirt road section. Dwight looked around, slightly confused by our destination . . . and I think a little worried.

I explained to him as we got off the bike and found a nearby bench, "This is my favorite spot in the whole of LA, Dwight. I come here to think, to meditate. I guess I come here to be inspired."

Dwight nodded as he looked out at the city below. The truth was that I didn't know anything about this man other than he had once been a truck driver. I asked him what he was doing now.

"Oh," he thought about it for a second before sitting down on the bench next to me, "I'm a student right now. Just keeping it simple, that's all. What's really cool is that when I first bumped into you, I was thinking, 'Oh this guy needs some help, so I'll just give it to him.' It's pretty cool to find out that it started something like this."

I wasn't sure how to explain what had happened. The long nights, the days dragging Kindness One across crowded dusty roads, the trips across continents and oceans, through killing fields, border crossings, fueled by kindness, adrenaline, and the amazing connections between strangers across the world.

Finally, I said, "It's been absolutely epic."

"I'm jealous," he replied, standing up and looking out over the edge of the cliff as he explained. "Right now, my journey has to be stagnant, you know? Certain journeys you can move, other journeys you have to stay in one place. But you? You were able to gradually move, so I'm jealous!"

I told Dwight about the gifts, but I explained, "It wasn't just that the gift helped to change that one person. But rather that maybe because their life was changed, they reached out and helped five people. And those five people helped five other people. And hundreds of people got to have another experience of this world because you were willing to help me."

Dwight tried not to smile, "All because of one tank of gas?"

We began to laugh, but I knew that he understood as well as I did that the whole world *can* be changed by one tank of gas.

Dwight sat back down, and I could tell that he was beginning to feel like he was part of this journey, that in some way, he had been with me the whole time. "Hopefully this will spread," he offered. "People need to start looking out for one another."

Spreading was exactly what I had in mind, and it was going to start with the man sitting right in front of me.

I told Dwight about all the people I had met and the gifts given — from the first gift to the most recent one. And then, I got to Dwight.

"There are some people who have kindness in their hearts and some people who don't," I told him. "And that's okay. But you strike me as someone who does, someone who has so much goodness."

"I try," he laughed nervously. "I try to keep that goodness. But it's really rough sometimes to keep your head above water."

I knew what he meant. Because though a river of kindness might flow between us, sometimes it's hard to swim in the undertow. We get sucked down by circumstance or by the consequences of our demons, and we forget that it's only by lifting out our hand to another that we are saved.

Finally, I asked Dwight the one thing I had wondered since we first met, "Why did you help me?"

He shrugged his shoulders, "Because you needed help."

Because you needed help.

I spoke some more about the trip and then reminded him of when he told me that he hoped to travel one day.

"Yeah, see for me, it's special. Because on one level, personally, it's something that I enjoy, to go see other cultures, be in other environments. But at the same time, it's professional because I'm training to be a psychologist, and it's a good way for me to learn what is different about those cultures."

"Really? So if you could travel the world, that would be like enrolling in the school of life."

"Oh wow, yeah. Very Kerouac-ian," he laughed. "Basically that would be it. LA is such a big city in such a small place, and there's more going on outside of it."

I understood. I had grown up in a big city that felt like a small place. And I had wondered what the world was like beyond it. I had dreamed of that world. And what I discovered was that I brought a piece of every place I visited home with me. A little part of India will always be in me. A little part of Vietnam. A little part of the Griffith Park Observatory.

I knew it was time to tell him why we were here.

"You know how you just talked about your desire to travel the world and go into the school of life and inspire other people and to learn and bring back what you learn to help others?"

"I would like to," he said wistfully, still not fully comprehending what was about to come.

"Well, you're going to get that chance."

"Me?" he said, looking like he had just been run over by his old truck.

"You. What I am going to do is I am going to pay for you to go on an around-the-world journey. Your hotels will be paid for, your spending money paid for, your flights paid for."

"Whoa. I didn't expect that."

"And one more thing."

"Yeah?"

"I want this journey to go full circle. So along with that worldwide trip, I am going to give you money to change someone's life. You can decide to change one person's life. You can decide to change five people's lives. But what you did to start this journey, I am now giving you the chance to do for someone else."

Silence.

"Wow. I'm speechless," he finally said.

He stood up again and looked back out across LA, as though he could now see beyond the edge of its horizon. He started to laugh, his eyes growing wet as he explained. "Nothing like this ever happens to me, so you have to understand that I don't run into situations like this at all. I've never gotten an opportunity before like this."

He muttered to himself, "Good things never happen to me."

How many times have we all believed that lie? That somehow we are fated for bad luck and hard times. That we're resigned to limit our dreams. We tell ourselves that the best stuff in life is for other people; that somehow *our* dreams are less deserving. But none of it is true. We are free to dream the impossible.

Dwight finally looked at me and smiled, "I'm tripping out, man. I don't believe you."

I showed him some photos of the other gifts I had given to people around the world as evidence that this was not a lie.

Finally, the truth began to sink in. "I can't wait to tell my mother," Dwight told me. "She's not going to believe it, either. Thank you so much. I feel like I'm sitting on top of the Himalayas right now."

"You will be, if you want," I replied. I watched as the words hit Dwight, as the shackles of his own self-doubt fell away and the whole world expanded before him. I drove him back to the coffee shop where we met. It was nearly six o'clock. Night would be falling soon, but I didn't need to worry about finding a place to stay. For the first time in months, I had already booked a spot.

And it was only four miles away. I drove back again through Hollywood and down Hollywood Boulevard, wondering if I might run into my friend and his sign. I couldn't find him, but maybe enough people had seen his sign. Maybe his work was done. As I drove up my street, I could feel my heart pounding in my chest. Sure, I had spoken to Lina sporadically over the course of the trip, but now I would be coming home, a slightly different man. And Lina would surely be a slightly different woman.

I wasn't sure what to expect, but I had

managed to cross three oceans and a world filled with heartbreaking beauty and generous connections; I think I could manage home. I knew that it was like Nora had said: the most important thing, the *only* important thing was love.

I drove into my driveway, took a deep breath, and walked into my house. Like Argos in Odysseus' story, the first thing that happened was my dog went nuts. At least he was happy to see me. Then Lina walked down the staircase and immediately melted into my arms. I held her tightly. This person had become the emergency contact of my journey, taking my calls from far-flung places. As much as adrenaline and connection had gotten me across the world, it was Lina's love that had gotten me home. I remembered Bill and Melissa's words about being best friends, and I knew that in my arms, I held mine.

The first words that came out of her mouth were, "I am so proud of you."

And that might have just been the final gift I was really waiting for. I burst into tears while embracing the woman I loved. She held me as I cried my eyes out, proud of what I had achieved. Proud of what I had experienced. And proud of humanity's goodness that had greeted me around this world of ours.

I thought giving the gift to Dwight would have brought my journey full circle, but I realized that the true start and the true end were right here, in my home, with the person I loved, knowing that the river of kindness flows between all of us, but the tides of love run deepest.

I was home.

EPILOGUE:
. . . OR WHAT HAPPENED
NEXT

"The next evolutionary step for
humankind is to move from
human to kind."
— Author Unknown

When I first left London to come to America, I had quit my job, sold my flat, and was leaving my family, and yet something inside me felt I was finally going home. I didn't know that Los Angeles would be my final destination. I probably would have laughed if you had told me as much, but as I woke up in my sunny bedroom that first morning after my return, I began to realize that the connections we make with those we love are the foundation for the rest of our work.

Over the next few weeks, I could barely move. I was physically, emotionally, and spiritually exhausted. I spent quality time with Lina and my friends, and, of course,

Winston, but I also spent a lot of time with me, still reeling from the magical, impossible journey that had just taken place.

Was I the same man who had left this beautiful city, or had I changed irrevocably? I just kept coming back to that moment in Pittsburgh when Tony gave me the new clothes he had received from the shelter. He had been concerned that I wouldn't have enough. A man with nothing had given me everything. And in that one act, he changed my life forever.

Because now that I was home, I wanted to see that moment replayed in so many of the choices in my life. I wanted to be the person who gave for no other reason than the fact that I cared enough to give. I didn't want to just connect; I wanted to be concerned. I wanted to be in communion, invested in the lives of others in a way that would forever echo the best of who we can be to each other. By simply holding the door open or going out of our way for someone we barely know, we send out a wave of energy into the world. And we touch each other.

And in that intimacy, we say in the quiet voice that once whispered to me, *I believe in you.*

Every time someone bought me a tank of

gas, those were the words that I heard. *I believe in you.* Every time someone offered me food or a place to stay, they were saying, *I believe in you.*

And I want you to know — yes you — that *I believe in you.*

It's in that connection that we find the strength to fulfill our dreams. We discover that our trials are worth bearing. Our gifts worthy of offering.

I didn't know that when I was sitting at my desk in that rainy London office. I thought dreams were fulfilled through self-will and determination. What I learned is that it takes a village to raise a dream. And for this dream, I got to meet the village that spans the world.

I knew that this journey couldn't end with me. I realized that on an individual basis, we all have the power to create change, but the true magic happens when that revolution expands to touch hundreds, thousands, millions of lives.

It was time for me to start another little revolution.

I kept the flame alive by giving the final gift to Dwight, but there was more I could do. I could hear my own voice now echoing: *Leon, there is more.*

Over the next few weeks, I started talking

to Lina about how I wanted to keep giving the gifts.

"To people around town?" she asked hesitantly. "Or across the world?"

"I'm not sure," I told her. "I mean, I think what I really want is to give people the gift of the trip I just took. I want other people to be able to give."

Not that she didn't have selfish reasons for agreeing, if that meant I might stick around for a bit, but Lina smiled as she said, "I think that's a great idea."

And that's exactly what I decided to do. I would start a charity that would enable young adults to go out and experience the world the same way that I had. But with a catch. They would spend ten days in a city, way, way out of their comfort zone. Think a slum in India, or a rural part of Peru. Maybe a refugee camp in Haiti. And there, they would be of service. Maybe they would work at an orphanage. Maybe they would work with a disaster relief group to save the lives of others.

But in addition, I would offer them the chance to change someone else's life. They would get to help someone else fulfill their dream — and they would choose who that person was and what the gift should be. They would document their journey on social media, and when they came home they would have to give speeches to their school or their college. Because we have to give it away in order to keep it. Just as I had seen the torch of kindness passed from one soul to the next, so I hoped that these students might be the first to light the flame, but certainly not the last. I decided to name the charity The Human Interaction Project (www.humaninteractionproject.org) because that was what it was all about. It was about dropping the mask, putting down the phone, reaching out to a complete stranger, and connecting in a way that forever changes us.

When I told Lina the name, she smiled. She reminded me of what she had said before I left: "Go and change the world, Leon."

I know I didn't change the world, but I hope that I left some small part of it feeling better. I started off with the vague idea of a dream, and along my route, I discovered an even bigger one lurking below. Because at the root of all our love, and the root of all our heartbreak, is that undying, unstoppable desire to be connected to each other. I believe we all want to live in that web of kindness, and not just because of what we receive by being a resident, but by what we are able to give.

After the monk walked away that morning in Big Sur, I looked at the actual river flowing in front of me. There were fallen tree limbs in it, jagged rocks, stones, and pebbles, and yet the water could not be dammed. Much like kindness. The river is flowing, my friends. Go take a swim.

WHERE ARE THEY NOW?

I am sure you are wondering what happened to the people whom I met along the way — including those not necessarily listed in this book. I made so many brief but incredible friendships, and each one fueled this journey. I wish I could have repaid everyone's kindness, but like Mother Teresa said, "It's not how much we give but how much love we put into giving." And from all of them, I learned to love.

Here is what happened to them after our meeting:

Willy and Chery went to England and attended their son's wedding, taking pictures and gracefully making a toast in my honor. Tony is living in his house in Pittsburgh and has attended culinary school in an effort to change his life. The transition from living on the streets to a far more normal life has not been without its challenges. But as I told Tony on the day I met him, he has a friend for life, one who will always be there for him as he was there for me.

Finesse and Tchale have recorded their music video and you can find it at www .tchaleandfinesse.com. Their music can brighten up even the darkest day, so if you are a famous music producer please go and visit their site. They continue to inspire.

Under the tutelage of Alex, Angelo has enrolled in fencing school, where he is learning from his master how to be a champion on the court *and* in life. Bekim and his family have a new cow, which Bekim has joked that they plan on calling Leon. I gently suggested this wouldn't be necessary, but there could be a cow named Leon roaming the hills of Montenegro right now! Though my small gift was only a drop in the ocean, Mehmet and Nasuh were able to use the funds to buy more equipment for their rescue workers, not only changing lives, but also saving them.

Dheeru is driving his new rickshaw around Delhi providing for his family. I have spoken with him a few times since our chance meeting, and hopefully one day I will take him up on his offer to drive me around town for free. Dilip's eldest son is enrolled in one of the best schools in Varanasi. His youngest son is still too young to attend school, but hopefully he will be inspired to follow in his brother's footsteps. Dilip, my friend, if you are reading this, you are still one of the best teachers your boys could ever find.

The kids at the Calcutta orphanage are no longer drinking unclean water. The purifiers were recently delivered, and that's now one less thing to worry about. In addition, they have received the sports equipment as well as a fully stocked library filled with stories that I hope might light up their imagination, as books have always done for mine. Seng and Mai are living in a proper house for the first time, which a local charity joined in helping build. The construction has just finished, and there will be no more rainy days to worry about. And in Vietnam, the doctor and his staff were able to provide one hundred eye surgeries to people in need, showing that sometimes the best place to use the gifts we learned abroad is right at home.

In Whistler, the dog shelter received all the goodies to cheer up the dogs *and* their human companions. And last but not least, Dwight is currently on his journey around the world, on a break from school. I often wonder whom he will meet, and how he will be changed by the connections he creates and the love I am sure he will find. I look forward to hearing his story when he returns.

A NOTE FROM THE AUTHOR

As I mention several times in the book, I was traveling with a film crew to document this journey. The crew's role was to hang back until I had made the personal connections myself, and only then emerge to document the moment. They were respectful and only came into the story as requested by me. *The Kindness Diaries* is my story of connection with people around the world, and I have made every effort to keep those encounters as genuine as possible without going into detail of what the crew was doing at any particular place and time. Suffice to say they had their own experiences (and plenty of their own stories), which are not in the scope of this book to detail.

ACKNOWLEDGMENTS

My journey across the world changed my life in many ways. I am eternally grateful to the people I met along the way — both the people who by now you are very familiar with, and the many, many more who were not mentioned in this book. Yet there is another category of friends and family who were absolutely integral to my journey. The people behind the scenes who without their love, support, and creativity you would not be reading this book.

I would like to thank my mother and father for their unwavering support for my decision to branch off on my own path. And my three brothers whose achievements always amaze me and whose friendship and love I cherish dearly.

Steve, Greg, James, and Erick, you know how much I appreciate every ounce of the heart and soul you put into this project. Thank you for believing in this crazy Englishman.

The good people at Reader's Digest: Thank you for your faith in me. Fiona, I guess some things are just meant to be. I am humbled by the belief you had in me and appreciate it more than you will ever know.

Suzanne, you are a wise and kind lady. You have taught me a lot and I thank you for your guidance.

My editor extraordinaire, Kristen. Without your creativity and your "magic sprinkles" this book would not be the book it is today. I owe you big time! Thanks for putting up with me over these past few months and I look forward to many more editorial adventures.

My good friend Alfa, I thank you for all your wise advice and all your help with the book. When you go to India, my good friend Ramchandra is waiting for you.

Winston. When I said in the book that you taught me how to love, I wasn't kidding. You did. And for that I will be forever grateful.

Last but not least, to my darling girlfriend, Lina. Sorry that I left you for all those months. I can't promise that I won't do it again, but I can promise that I will love you deeply along the way. I am forever grateful that our paths crossed. You are a shining beacon in my stormy sea. I love you.

ABOUT THE AUTHOR

Leon Logothetis is a TV host, producer, author, traveler and all around good guy. Formerly a London broker, he gave up his comfortable life to travel and find real human connection. He is the host of "The Amazing Adventures of A Nobody" which was licensed to National Geographic International and aired in over 100 countries, including in the United States on Fox Reality Channel and Canada's OLN. He is also the author of a book by the same title. He has appeared on Good Morning America, CNN, FOX, BBC among other mainstream media outlets. He runs a production company called Principal Media and lives in Los Angeles, CA with his dog Winston.

JA